About the autho

Chuck Spezzano,
counsellor, trainer, visionary
leader. He holds a Psychology. From
30 years of counselling perience and 26 years of
psychological research and seminar leadership,
Dr Spezzano and his wife, Lency, created the
breakthrough therapeutic healing model Psychology of
Vision. The impact of this model has brought deep
spiritual, emotional and material change to thousands
of participants from around the world.

Also by Chuck Spezzano

If It Hurts, It Isn't Love
Wholeheartedness
50 Ways to Find True Love
50 Ways to Let Go and Be Happy
50 Ways to Get Along with Absolutely Anyone

50 Ways to Change Your Mind and Change The World

CHUCK SPEZZANO, Ph.D.

HODDER
MOBIUS

Copyright © 2002 by Chuck Spezzano

First published in Great Britain in 2002 by Hodder and Stoughton
A division of Hodder Headline

The right of Chuck Spezzano to be identified as the Author of the Work
has been asserted by him in accordance with the Copyright, Designs and
Patents Act 1988.

1 2 3 4 5 6 7 8 9 10

A CIP catalogue record for this title is available from the British Library.

ISBN 0 340 79354 6

Typeset by Palimpsest Book Production Limited,
Polmont, Stirlingshire
Printed and bound in Great Britain by
Clays Ltd, St Ives plc

Hodder and Stoughton
A division of Hodder Headline
338 Euston Road
London NW1 3BH

This book is dedicated to Peter and Sherry
in love, laughter and delight.

Contents

Acknowledgements

I would like once again to acknowledge the living influence of *A Course in Miracles* in my life. In 1977, I prayed for a book to take me all the way home. I was told about *A Course in Miracles* and referred to it a short time afterwards. Nothing has taught me more about the nature of the mind, transformation and reality, or helped me more personally. Much of what I have learned has become a part of this book – learning that has been enhanced and developed from what I have learned from my wife and children, from my clients, and the many new methods that *A Course in Miracles* inspired.

I would like to acknowledge Jeremy Roe for his *5 Why* method, which I have found to be something more than just a source of information. When extended a little further, it has become a major healing tool.

I would also like to acknowledge Brian Mayne, Jane Corcoran, Donna Francis, Pat Saunders, Rowan Malcolm and Bonnie Close for their editing skills in the first stage of this book and Sue Allen, Heidi Ainsworth, Peggy Chang and Karen Sullivan when the book was rewritten and lengthened.

Finally, I would like to acknowledge my children Chris and J'aime, and my wife Lency, for their deep and continuing love and support, and for sharing me so generously with others in my work. I couldn't do it without you.

Getting Started

This book may seem very different to you. You may not be accustomed to reading books that claim to be able to change your life, but even if you are, you'll find something unique here. A book that purports to change your world must be different, and it must use a different language to encourage you to see things in a different way. And that's the crux of my approach. The old way simply hasn't worked. New ideas are essential when a different model is presented, to open a new world and a unique way of thinking. If you have enough curiosity, interest or motivation, you will begin to learn and use this model. It is one which can show you the way to change your feelings, mind and world.

My experience as a therapist, counsellor, consultant and life coach for over 30 years has taught me that we can change the world around us by changing our minds. This book presents and explains the core dynamics which come together to produce all problems, as well as the basic principles that can heal such problematic dynamics. When used properly, any one of these principles can collapse your problem and literally change your life.

The beauty of the methods described here is that they give us back our power. Some people find it reassuring to clutch on to the belief that they are victims. They do so because they are afraid of their own minds and their power. The tens of thousands of experiences that I have had clearly indicate that when people realise that they are ultimately responsible for the problems in their lives, they find choices. And as they realise their choices, it becomes a turning point for them to change even seemingly impossible problems. And it hasn't just happened once. It's happened time after time, and on every occasion.

Conversely, I have found that if people don't want to change then they will not understand the healing principle, method or technique because they don't want to understand it. They don't *will* themselves to get over the problem because they are somehow still invested in it, stuck in the belief that it will give them something.

The power of the mind is magnificent in creating change. If we understand the nature of the problem, how it works, its purpose in our lives and how it fails to give us what we want, then we can make other choices. If our desire to change and heal is greater than our fear, we find a way to do it because we want it with all of our hearts.

After practising as a therapist for six years, I discovered *A Course in Miracles*, which corroborated much of what I believed, at the time, to be my own original findings. But it also spoke of other principles, which I began to explore and research. Some of the principles described in *A Course in Miracles* were not found in any of the psychology books I had read. I recognised these to be true in practical and transformational ways. I could and did use them to help free and heal people. Natural extensions of these principles became effective methods and techniques for therapeutic use in coaching, counselling and workshops.

Over the years, it has become ever clearer to me that there are certain negative dynamics – such as fear, guilt, loss and revenge – which work together to generate all manner of problems. If any one of these dynamics is truly transformed, problems collapse. If we learn to collapse our problems, whether they are large or small, we improve our lives and empower ourselves.

As we heal the problems and issues before us, we graduate to being able to face, handle and resolve even more challenging ones. Having learned the lesson of the old problems, nothing can stop us. As the old problems are resolved, our self-confidence grows in such a way that we are then ready for new and bigger issues.

The teachings in this book are based on the workings of the mind and emotions, and focus on how to change them. The premise is very simple: if they are changed, behaviour is automatically shifted. What's more, when the mind and emotions are altered, there comes about a shift in the world around us. So these principles are not only for resolving problems, but also for living in an empowered and transformational way, helping yourself and others. This book reflects my desire to make these principles more accessible to the many who can apply them to graduate from their present problems and to those dedicated others who will use these principles to completely transform their lives.

Using these principles not only helps us and those we love, but it radiates benefits out to the world at large. The world is always blessed when anyone is empowered and transformed to a new level of success and responsiveness, after having been stuck in the victim's wooden or reactive stance of fear, guilt, pain and recrimination.

While it may seem presumptuous to say that any problem can be healed in any one of 50 Ways, the nature of the mind's ability to free itself is such that this statement is completely true. We have a primordial legacy of truth, transformation, transcendence and miracles that can be drawn on to help remedy our life situations. Some problems heal immediately, size or difficulty notwithstanding. The ability to heal, and the speed at which we heal, seems to be tied to our willingness to move through the fear of change and to live at a whole new level of success. The amount of time it will take us to heal, or to move on to the next level is individual – in a nutshell, it takes as long as we believe it will take or as long as it takes us to gain the confidence to live at the whole next level. I have seen catastrophic illnesses disappear quickly while lesser problems have taken weeks.

The foundation of these healing principles is the belief that every problem is an illusion. Of course, when we are trapped in a problem, our suffering doesn't feel like an illusion. We can feel helpless and hopeless. However, if we don't change our problems by changing our thoughts and feelings about them, ourselves and others, they could even become our final conflicts.

I have seen these principles work time and again, both professionally and personally. When a major, or chronic, problem is being healed, it may, at first, seem as if the situation is getting worse. This is because many problems are layered and the more deeply we work the worse it can feel. But when it seems to be getting worse, it is actually getting better, much like a boil seems worse when we first lance it. Feeling worse, however, may be what moves us on the road to release and healing. A problem may sometimes have hundreds of layers. The positive choices we make for love, forgiveness, letting go, trust and blessing, lead us layer by layer in our healing process – and further along our personal evolution. On the other hand, if we transform one of the core dynamics, the whole problem can collapse.

We all know the frustration and distress we feel when we have a problem. At some time or other we have been on our proverbial knees with any number of problems, yet problems can motivate us to move in the right direction, to learn, change, grow and, as a result, heal and stay young. For in truth, we are always moving towards a greater life or towards death.

None of the thoughts that generate our feelings and actions are neutral. They are either life-enhancing or they carry us towards death. As we grew up we became responsible for our behaviour and reached a certain level of maturity. If we continue to grow, there comes a point where we also take responsibility for our emotions. This allows for true and successful partnership and brings about the balance of our masculine and feminine sides. Finally, we take responsibility for our thoughts, realising that they generate our world and the experiences we have as a result. This leads to mastery. At each level we have more integrity and become more open, responsive, loving and powerful. The more we assume responsibility for our own lives and for changing them accordingly, the more we are able to help others.

Because any problem is a signal that we are being called upon to change our lives, it also follows that the greater the problem, the greater the change or birth that calls us. We don't have to know *how* to change our lives because we will be shown a way if we are willing. We don't even have to know what the change will look like, as that too will come to us in time. We only have to want and choose with our whole hearts for the change to occur. A problem is the result of a conflict coming from a split mind. What we want with our whole hearts both becomes a prayer for help and resolves the conflict of the mind. What touches our heart motivates us and when motivation occurs, change occurs naturally.

Because of the nature and constancy of problems, this book is intended to be a companion, always available when needed. Hopefully the healing principles it describes will naturally become a part of your way of life. Do this and you will not see problems as signs of suffering and death, but as opportunities and motivation to bring about birth and peace. This book comes from a desire to give you inside information in a transformational world. Use these principles and they can become life-long friends.

I wish you courage and great good fortune in your life.

May all of your births be easy ones.

Chuck Spezzano, PhD
Hawaii
October, 2001

Blockbusting and Accountability

The answers in this book are not theoretical; they are practical, part and parcel of what I have learned over thirty years and now keep in my healing toolbox. They are undoubtedly effective. I have found that when the mind is healed of conflict and we are at peace, the answers we need in order to act come to us. When enough change accumulates in the mind, a shift in our world is automatic. Sometimes this can occur immediately.

Back in the 1970s I was a psychologist working for the US Navy doing drug rehabilitation. Our centre was faced with the reality of budget cuts and an eventual loss of 75 percent of rehabilitation time. This caused our results which, at the time, were the best rehabilitation results in the world, to plummet. The therapists there, both military and civilian, decided to get better rather than give up. This motivated me to embark even further on an exploration of principles that were fast and effective in therapy and to discover principles that could make changes in what was then described as one of the hardest populations to help, let alone change – adolescent drug abusers.

After fifteen years of therapeutic work I began to see that every situation was the result of a choice on our part; if the original choice is uncovered, it can be made again. This was personally mind-blowing because I had been a victim often enough in my own life. I began to see that being a victim was the result of these self-defeating patterns within us, and that these patterns put us in the weakest position possible. But I also found that they could be changed easily enough if there was willingness.

This book is based on the concepts of personal responsibility and choice, which empower change and accountability. If we are not responsible for our situations and our lives, we can only feel like victims, carrying grievances and remaining stuck in the problem. We become part of the problem, passing on the pain directly or withdrawing, and passing on the pain indirectly, instead of being part of the solution.

Here is one dramatic example of a woman who took total responsibility, and was able to change seemingly impossible situations as a result. Twenty-five years ago I was leading a series of evening workshops in San Diego for professional enhancement and support called 'Personal Power'. One woman in the workshop was a master of social work who dealt with abused children. Her chief concern was her obesity. I learned that her job was extremely stressful and emotionally demanding, and she was handling the stress by eating.

She said, 'When I come home, I can't talk to my husband who is away with the navy. I can't unload on my own child, who is only six, so I go to the refrigerator for comfort. My husband is with the fleet off the coast of Iran, and we've received word that no one will be coming back from the fleet for two years.'

The woman clearly needed something more than just the support we were giving her, so I asked her if she'd like to go deeper.

She replied, 'Absolutely, I'm getting desperate. I need something.'

Even though we all knew she wanted her husband home, I asked her to pretend that she didn't want her husband home. And if she didn't want him home, why would that be?

She replied, 'Oh, that's easy. When my husband is home he pretends he's my commanding officer. He tries to rule the roost, disregarding my input. I have a professional degree and he is only a petty officer, yet he treats me like a child.'

At this point I suggested some more effective forms of communication and dealing with the problem. I then asked if she had the courage to share her feelings with her husband honestly, without blame. She could then begin to deal with their marriage issue and her feelings of emotional abuse, which were echoed in the physical abuse of the children with whom she worked.

'Absolutely!' she replied. 'I would much rather have him home to work this out than banish him for such a long time.'

The next week in the evening workshop the woman immediately raised her hand to share. As I called on her she blurted out, unable to contain her excitement, 'You know that no one was due to leave the fleet off of Iran for two years because of the crisis? The most amazing thing has occurred. They are sending six men home from the fleet and my husband is one of them. He'll have shore-side duty here for the next six years.'

This dramatic change may seem unbelievable to you but it has become an everyday experience for me.

Personal Responsibility and Choice

To choose to be responsible and therefore able to respond and change goes beyond the judgement and guilt that locks us in. I began to see glimpses of this truth in my fourth year as a therapist and it took me almost fifteen years to realise that time and again we choose what happens to us. We commonly make choices that are reflected in the stories we continually tell about what is happening to us. When we make choices, we do so because we think it will bring us happiness. When we consider the stories we tell to friends, family and acquaintances it might dawn on us that we are telling these stories for a purpose. Our stories are always an attempt to get or prove something.

Here are a few other key dynamics that are part of every problem:

- We create traps to protect our fears.
- We use others' attacks on us and the unfairness in life to try to pay off our guilt.
- We create pain to beg for help or try to get our needs met.

- We attempt to take and end up losing.
- We win the competition, even if it is to become the best of the worst.
- We have things done to us physically, which we are doing to others on an emotional, mental or metaphoric level. We reap what we sow.
- We have painful things happen to us so we seem forced to do what we wanted to do all along.
- We hurt ourselves or become victimised to get back at others.
- We have people act out the shadow figures (see page 321) of our mind to delude ourselves into thinking it has nothing to do with us.
- We are victimised so we can attack while appearing innocent.
- We sacrifice ourselves in suffering in an attempt to save someone close to us.

In every problem, no matter what the dynamic, we are trying to achieve happiness through means that could never work, such as taking, attacking, revenge, defending, repaying debts or making up for guilt.

In all of these cases, the outcome will not make us happy. All of us make similar choices every day and then hide them from ourselves. Healing ourselves is becoming aware of what we have denied and making choices that work.

Soon after learning the principle of accountability, which is being totally accountable without blaming others, I saved myself from a major accident. As I drove along the highway, I realised that

I was mesmerised and in an intensely erotic mood. I became aware of myself as I wiped the sweat from my brow and moved my seat back from the steering wheel to give myself more room. Fortunately I had just enough awareness to examine myself in this process. I asked myself what was happening and when I looked inside to see what was there, I saw my car smashed and on fire against a bridge abutment further down the road. Later I realised that I was attempting to put myself in the hospital as a way to try to get my ex-girlfriend back. Attempts to get something in this fashion always have haphazard results. For instance, the accident may have been fatal or my ex-girlfriend may never have heard I was in the hospital because we had a different circle of friends, to mention just two of many possibilities. Obviously I had a split mind about being with her or we would never have broken up in the first place, but losing her had triggered grief strong enough for me to attempt to hurt myself to bring her back.

Numerous other people I have worked with have reported saving themselves from suffering and accidents by catching themselves just before they did something self-destructive.

Past Disguised as the Present

Unless we are totally present – in which case we are vibrant, successful, happy and joyful – some past pattern is programming our lives and experience. We carry old baggage and wounds, all of which keep coming up disguised as a present problem for the purpose of healing. Our present problems are mostly made up of past, unhealed problems and, if they are not resolved when they show up in the present, they become compounded.

As we react because of the past emotional baggage in our present problems, we are weighed down, drained of our energy and we react to illusions, which began in the past, as we attempt to handle the present situation. Worse yet, we respond to the present situation as if it were the past and this can cause us to misstep. We all have different coping mechanisms and defences, from hysteria, repression and overreaction to dissociation and compensation. None of these strategies will work or supply more than a short-term benefit and they will all become part of a long-term problem.

Attempting to get is a defence

In many ways we can say that all of our problems are defences that attempt to protect us by separating us. Whether we are babies or grandparents, we tend to try to get something from others or from life when we have lost bonding, our emotional connective force, which creates love and success with ease. This separation or fractured bonding results in fear, misunderstandings, loneliness, loss and needs. These are the cornerstones to any problems. We use *getting* as a defence to make up for this, but we end up creating more loss. No one wants to be in a relationship where a partner is always trying to get something from us.

The more someone tries to take, the more we pull back.

Our attitude becomes one of grasping or acquisitiveness to win some form of happiness outside ourselves. Seeking outside ourselves leads to a cycle of disappointment, hurt, withdrawal and giving up, then searching and being disappointed again. Attempting to get turns our lives into loss after loss – or momentary pleasure for something we begin to value less and less because our value comes from what we give, not what we take.

Loss, if not mourned and healed, will be compensated by roles. These can never be successful since they cover over the original loss or trauma. The three main roles are Neediness, Independence (in which we act as if things really don't matter or affect us), and the Untrue Helper (where we hide loss by trying to take care of others as a way of hiding from ourselves and our feelings).

Being a victim and payoffs

Being a victim can grow to be a constant, recurring theme in our lives. Even deeper than the victim trap is the victim story, where we write chapter after chapter on how someone has done things to us against our will. The victim stance, and even the tragedies underwriting it, subconsciously hides our own violence, attack and revenge, while calling for love and help under the guise of being victimised. Being a victim actually serves certain purposes and agendas which we choose and then repress.

The purpose of a problem is that it is a payoff for something we are trying to get. Typically it justifies and allows us to do something we've always wanted to do or it gives us an excuse not to do what we haven't wanted to do. With the solution of a problem comes understanding and awareness. This is a choice in the right direction, which will build our lives.

Here is a quick categorisation of some of the core purposes of being a victim, which are often at work simultaneously. If one of these dynamics is collapsed through healing the whole problem can dissolve.

- Getting a certain need met
- Calling for someone's help or attention
- Paying off guilt
- Getting revenge
- Using an excuse to not have to do something
- Justifying what we want to do
- Becoming independent
- Attacking another
- Getting others to sacrifice
- Controlling
- Not facing the fear of the next step or the fear of a gift, talent or opportunity
- Proving we are worthy through sacrificing ourselves
- Trying to save others through our sacrifice
- Holding on to an indulgence
- Holding onto someone or something

We make split-second decisions and if the decision is negative, we bury or repress it. In most cases,

when our decisions for negative experiences are
brought back into awareness, we can easily make
new positive choices. When examined, these strategies or manipulations to try to get what we want,
which is ultimately happiness, just won't work.
Because I am aware of this, I sometimes catch myself
deciding to have a cold or the flu in an attempt to
get some payoff, such as attention, love or rest.
Having caught myself, I realise that these are poor
decisions which won't work because of the 'element
of taking', and I immediately make other, more
positive decisions. When we catch ourselves making
negative decisions, we can just change our minds.
Similarly, we can go back to the root of a problem-
situation where we made a negative decision, and
come to a new choice and understanding. When we
go back and remake these decisions and re-establish
the bonding, the result is a major transformative
effect.

The two major payoffs

Denial, dissociation and repression hide our guilt
and pain. Usually we keep the dark pieces of our
minds buried in secrecy; however, there are many
ways to describe two of the bottom-line purposes
of all of our problems. To help discover and explore
core dynamics, I have described a number of them
in this book. In my experience two of the major
payoffs for any problem are specialness and dissociated or untrue independence. The latter is the
separation caused by the authority conflict (see Way
45) or the rebel shadow figure (see Way 45). The

other core dynamic is specialness (see Way 37), which is the desire to have our needs met so that we are acknowledged as special or best. This aspect wants glamour and attention, even if it has to be the 'dark' glamour of a problem. This sets up the competition, which encourages the vicious circle of superiority–inferiority, but never the equality that makes for successful relationships. This dissociated independence is our mistaken idea of freedom, which we use when we are actually frightened of freedom and we set up heartbreak and burnout as an excuse to have it.

Specialness sets up a shrine around us wanting to make us the one and only. All of our upsets come from not being treated in some special way. In other words, if we are offended or feel bad in any way, we believe that someone has not treated us right. This generates an automatic grievance that locks us into a problem. It is only a matter of time before hurt, anger and resentment surface and the honeymoon turns into a fight, or, as *A Course in Miracles* puts it, our special love relationship turns into a special hate relationship.

The desire to be 'independent' and 'special' blocks responsibility, partnership, interdependence, equality, intimacy, happy relationships and success. Independence is the hidden agenda of the ego, which always needs to be the boss and the special one. Time and again we hide this from our awareness. If we become conscious of these elements we can let them go in favour of more successful choices and better investments. We would not continue to pour good money into financial investments that have gone sour, yet we do it all the time in our everyday lives, emotions, relationships and careers. It is time to realise our power to change our minds and use them for greater success in life.

Change, Blessed Change

Let me give you an example of how change, or the movement forward to a new level of truth, frees and opens up our lives to a new level of abundant living. When I first visited England in 1983, I was working with a woman by the name of Mary who was a 75-year-old widow. She began to talk about her mother and her belief that her mother didn't want her. This had been the heartbreak of her life. As she spoke, her 77-year-old best friend was encouraging her to discuss this issue more.

I asked Mary, 'If you were to know when you began to believe that your mother didn't want you, it probably happened at the age of . . . ?'

'Ten', she replied.

I said, 'If you were to know what was going on that led you to believe you weren't wanted, it was probably . . . ?'

She said, 'My mother scolded me very strongly.'

I asked her if she had personally scolded anyone in her life, and she laughed and said, 'Yes. Quite a few.'

'Did that mean you didn't love or want them?' I asked.

'Oh no', she replied. 'It was always those closest to me that I scolded or complained to!'

'What was going on with you when you scolded them?'

She said, 'The times I scolded the worst was when I was afraid for them.'

So I asked, 'When your mother scolded you so strongly, was it that she didn't like you, or was she afraid for you?'

At my question Mary began to weep happy tears, saying, 'I can see it now. She likes me. She loves me. She was just afraid for me. Oh, all these years I thought she didn't want me.'

I asked, 'Can you let in all of her love now?'

'Yes! Oh, yes!' she cried.

And so change, blessed change had come to Mary after 65 years of carrying the pain of misunderstanding.

It was time for tea, and I'll never forget the sight of those two silver-haired ladies walking arm-and-arm ahead of me down the hall, crying with joy.

Change inside equals change outside

Years ago, when I heard the song *We Are the World* I knew from experience that it wasn't just a song, but also a principle of truth. The world and we are intrinsically bound and it reflects our choices, fear and guilt. This principle can be used to create change quickly. It also introduces other principles, such as reciprocity. As Christ said: 'You reap what you sow!' What we do to others we do to ourselves, or, 'People who live in a house of mirrors should not throw stones.' The mirror of the world reflects our mind and our problems in the world reflect conflicts within us.

Psychology is the fastest of the slow ways to change. The word psychology is itself derived from the Greek words *psyche*, meaning 'the mind' or 'the soul', and *logos*, meaning 'the word' or 'study'. Grace and miracles, which are always available to us, can generate change much faster than psychology.

One of the first principles I learned, and it seemed almost magical in its transformative effect, is that the inner and outer worlds are inextricably connected. The outer world is a reflection of the inner. Change in the microcosm of one's mind has an effect on the macrocosm. Problematic or troublesome people, problems, illnesses and situations can change in an easy and blessed way as inner healing takes place, bringing about a new perception that can transform the world. At some level all transformation is a change of perception.

Unchanged pain, old separations or traumas become problem patterns and our choices at those times become fixed beliefs. Fixed negative beliefs have the same effect as continuously making negative choices. These beliefs, most of which we are unaware of, determine not only how we experience the situation, but determine the situation itself.

Our minds have a direct effect on the world and the world reflects what is within our minds, reinforcing our beliefs. This can become a vicious circle where we are always compounding mistaken and thus illusionary and painful perceptions. As we become motivated to change, we somehow find another way. As a result, changing our mind can change our world. I found that as people change their minds, there is an effective outward change because the world mirrors our thoughts and choices. I began to see this as a principle rather than as a theory, and time and again I have been able to use it in a practical way to help free people. When a client and I successfully joined and found the root of the problem, outer symptoms disappeared without the client necessarily needing to change behaviour. The change had already been brought about by our healing work. Often other people with troublesome situations were completely transformed by the time they reached their home. This is one of the benefits of working directly in the subconscious mind.

Another dramatic example I had in my formative learning years occurred in a teenage workshop I led in San Diego. Given the number of attendees, and the natural resistance of the age group, I worked with many of the co-facilitators in leading the small groups and two supervisors who visited the small groups assigned to them. I facilitated the large group and also spent time visiting all of the small groups. We used music as a medium to get people in touch with what they were feeling and to open up the sharing. About three-quarters of the way through the workshop, I was approached by one of the female group leaders and a young man who was her supervisor. They asked for help with a 14-year-old girl whose face seemed completely lifeless.

The group facilitator said she had not been able

to connect with or animate the young woman. When the supervisor visited, he had not even been able to engage the young woman in conversation. In the next large group meeting I addressed the young woman at an appropriate time.

I asked her, 'Sylvia, do you realise how dead you seem?'

For the first time in the whole training she showed some real feeling. As I spoke these words, a smile opened her whole face and she said, 'Yeah. I know'. She continued smiling.

I thought, Whoa! We've got someone with a major death wish here. I then asked her, 'Do you want to die?'

She replied, 'Ever since I can remember, I've had a dream of Dracula waving me to come to him as he stands over a gravestone. I run to him, and as I get closer I realise that the gravestone has my name on it. I'm running as fast as I can, but still I'm going very slow in the dream and I always wake up before I get to him.'

'What is it that makes you want to die?' I asked.

'When I was three years old my twin was very, very sick, and all night I prayed for God to take me instead, because my sister was the good one', she said.

Try as I might from a number of approaches, there seemed to be nothing I could do to influence her to change her desire to die. We then had a break before we were to have the last two sets of music, followed by the last two sets of sharing. At this time, I had a conference with her therapist and supervisor.

I said, 'There's only one thing more I can think of for you to try. Look inside yourselves to see where you buried a desire to die.'

Both of them looked somewhat askance at me, for they were both young and vibrant. They also both assured me that they were willing to do anything if it would help the girl in their charge.

In the next set of music I glanced over to her therapist, just as the realisation of where she wanted to die came into her eyes. In seconds she was sobbing her heart out. I looked over at the girl and saw that for the first time she was crying and letting in the loving support. During the next sharing her group facilitator shared her own experience. When she was 18 years old, her recently married sister, who was her angel in the family, was killed with her husband in a fiery head-on collision by a drunk driving in the wrong lane.

During this sharing I looked over at Sylvia and realised that she had come halfway alive, but still she had another half to go. Soon after we began the last set of music, their supervisor, a friend of mine, looked over at me with a glance that said, 'I'm the most alive person I know, but if it'll help Sylvia, I'll find this last piece in me to help her.' It was only five minutes into the music when he erupted with pain, crying for all he was worth and being comforted by those beside him. As I looked over to the girl, I could see that she was also free, finally crying openly, and again accepting the help around her and letting the love in. During the sharing, my friend spoke of a scene that came into his mind from when he was three years old.

He said he had come up to his parents' bedroom door and found it closed. Because it was never closed, he opened the door and stared in horror as he found his mother, who was a surgical nurse, staring intently at her wrist with a scalpel. She then hollered at him for coming into the room when the door was closed, but he knew inside himself what was going on. In a moment he took on and 'swallowed' all the emotional pain that was in her.

One of the most poignant scenes of my life was seeing Sylvia, the group facilitator and her supervisor in the last session, crying and laughing in each other's arms.

Where our world seems immovable, implacable, painful, stuck or dead, it shows guilt, fear, revenge, judgement, grievance, indulgence, ambivalence and conflict hidden inside. When any one of these issues is transformed, it has an effect on all of them and there is a corresponding shift in the world around us. We then move forward until the next block stops us.

If we become too stuck, weighed down with problems, disappointed or conflicted, where we just want to die, then grace, healing, or blessed change is the answer. This can happen through:

- our desire to change
- our choice and willingness to go forward
- learning and, more importantly, unlearning
- understanding, acceptance, forgiving or giving
- letting go or integrating our conflicted mind
- our desire for the truth

- acknowledging our mistakes
- commitment and/or joining
- service to others
- love
- forgiveness of self and others

We bring about change, blessed change, as we break through where the ego has us stymied, an ego whose aim is to keep us from our purpose and the evolution that would break down its walls bit by bit.

Problem-solving

Here are just a few of the principles that can help in solving our problems:

- Any problem represents a conflict within our mind.
- Changing our mind equals changing our world.
- Problems are the result of mistaken choices and bad investments. We can make new, more enlightened choices.
- Every problem has a purpose.
- When the desire to heal or the willingness to move forward becomes stronger than the problem, it falls away.
- A problem represents a fear of the next step in our lives. Confidence for the next step represents the end of the problem.
- A problem reflects separation or lack of bonding. When joining occurs through love or forgiveness, the problem falls away.
- A problem comes from a grievance or judgement. When we decide to forgive, we are both freed.

Humans need purpose

We human beings are purposeful creatures. We
dream up our lives and what happens to us because
our lives and everything in them has a certain purpose. Any positive or negative event has a purpose
or payoff for us. Psychiatry has typically described
negative events as having *secondary* agendas or benefits. I found that these are not just secondary
agendas; for the most part they are our basic human
agendas. Transforming these human agendas is a
primary key to having the problem resolve and disappear. Either our egos or our higher minds can
guide and thus determine the purpose and outcome
of an event. The ego's goal is to build itself up and
make *itself* happy, while the higher mind seeks to
heal us and make *us* happy. If the ego guides the
event, it builds its own specialness and attacks those
who seem to threaten it, including the subconscious
attack we make through being a victim. It aims to
have the most and be the most special in some way.
If the guidance of the higher mind is followed, there
is love, sharing, helping, healing and answering the
call of our purpose.

Awareness versus ego

With awareness we are able to see that we are responsible for our lives because, if nothing else, we are
the constant factor in the lives that we have. We also
get to see that we hide certain choices we have made
because they would be unacceptable to our conscious mind. The ego tries to keep us from being

aware of our part in any situation. It fears responsibility and equality, feeling it would be damaging to its agenda of specialness, attack, vulnerability, the superior-inferior vicious circle and victimisation. It sees awareness as dangerous to the separation it needs to survive. Whenever we are victimised the ego is reinforced. The ego is the principle of separation, fear, competition, defensiveness and delay, whereas with awareness there is a flowing forward, an evolution and a joining.

The ego uses guilt as the primary weapon to keep us from looking inside. It warns us not to look inside where we would find things about ourselves so dark that no one could love us. It's true that we have buried guilt inside us, which paints a very black picture of who we are. Even the nicest people are compensating for shadow figures, which are mistaken beliefs of self-hatred. Yet for this guilt the ego demands self-attack at the very least, always self-punishment and if not yet, the soon-to-be sentence of death. While guilt is completely self-destructive, it is also an illusory mistake that serves the ego's purpose. Guilt actually reinforces the problem, resulting in the ego's continuation and, of course, the continuation of the problem itself. Guilt is one of the best adversaries against change and is frequently used when we are afraid of the next step.

Miracles can happen

One of the key aspects of healing is the acknowledgement that we are the one dreaming the dream or telling the story that becomes our lives. We can acknowledge that the problems and hidden choices that brought about our problems are a mistake and that they will never bring about the happiness we somehow thought they would. This is our story, our dream, and we can choose how it unfolds, and how we perceive it. We can look at it in a different way, or tell it in a different way, and it is then changed.

We can ask to be shown the way, we can ask to let go of the grievances that would open us for heaven's help in our current situation. When this occurs our mind is open to receive the miracles that release our suffering and are always waiting to be received as the solution heaven has for us.

This book is an acknowledgement that miracles can happen in our lives and that grace is always available to us. It demonstrates what can be done to reverse or undo mistakes we've made, such as taking revenge or holding onto grievances by thinking that it would make us happy. Every time we correct a mistake or let go of an illusion, our suffering falls away and finds an echo in the world as other pain and illusions that are graced by our healing melt away.

Using This Book

This book is meant to be an adventure, sharing principles that can help you as they have helped thousands of people. It will show you a new way of seeing the world that will enhance your power and confidence. As these principles filter into your life, you will find your life changing and you will find yourself beginning to move through limitations. As you graduate from problems and move on, you will find that more challenging problems await you, but your success, confidence and happiness will always grow. You will move through stage to stage, from problems to issues, from victim traps to relationship traps, from relationship traps to family traps and from family traps to soul (unconscious) traps. This book can be used repeatedly to assist you in your evolution at every stage of your healing process.

All at once, or one day at a time

This book can be used in many ways. You can read all 50 'Ways' at once to deepen and broaden your chances of success, or use one Way, one day at a time, cumulatively. While each Way is meant to be complete in itself, each one builds on the others, bringing together a new understanding. Because the lessons are set up incrementally, you can begin to develop your understanding of the whole picture of how our minds work – either to heal or hold ourselves up – as you venture further in the book. The more you concentrate and give yourself to the Ways the more they will be helpful to you. Each Way contains a principle that can free you from your problems. This book is meant to take you to a new level each time you undertake the adventure of it. As you let the principles sink into you, they will become part of your life.

Your most important lesson

As you become familiar with this book, and even before you start, you could just intuitively guess which Way from 1 to 50 contains the most important lesson to resolve your problem. Choosing one Way seems to get right at the core issue involved in your problem.

Letting the universe decide

If you become familiar with the Ways and their numbers, you can put the numbers in a hat and pick one(s), asking for the one that would best serve you to rid you of your problem(s). Usually one lesson is enough, but three (an ancient numerical symbol of transformation) might be used once you have become familiar with all of the lessons.

The way through

You have probably come into this book to empower yourself to change your life, and to move through the snags that ensnare you. This book is intended to renew and strengthen you by providing principles and healing exercises that can release you from your problems. Remember that this book is not just meant to be read; it is intended to be employed and used. As you give yourself to the exercises, you will be rewarded. As you no longer delay yourself behind the conflict, dilemma or pitfall, this book will assist you to move forward to a new level of confidence, success and intimacy.

In truth, all that is needed is your desire to wake up, to know what it is that you have hidden and to know that you have the power to free yourself. Our desire to love, know ourselves and others and our desire to awaken to a new world gives us the courage to face what we've been so frightened to examine, what we have denied, dissociated and repressed. In facing our buried issues, we open ourselves to inspiration, and to embrace long-lost gifts that were hidden along with our issues.

You don't need to believe the principles for them to be effective. If you already believed in the principles, you wouldn't have your present problems. For those who already live by these principles, this book is an excellent reminder of ways to heal the problems that emerge.

Good luck and all the best to you on your learning and healing adventure.

WAY 1 Learning the Lesson

Every problem has within it a certain lesson to be learned. Once the lessons are learned in a particular area of our lives there are typically no major problems to surprise us. On the other hand, if we don't learn the specific lessons set up for us in problems, they become a trial – a chronic problem in our lives from which we will suffer. Wherever we have become rigid or adamant, unwilling to learn or change, we will suffer. At one level, life is a school set up by our souls to learn certain lessons and to give certain gifts. These lessons are put before us in a timely manner and if we refuse to learn them our stress and pain grow accordingly. If we act righteously and in denial, pretending as if we know the answers, we are showing our unwillingness to learn or change. Willingness to learn opens our minds and sets us in a forward flow.

There are whole areas of the world where people are distrustful of learning and react against education of any kind. Of course, some education is really just preparing people for the job market, but even this will increase someone's confidence and expand their mind. The education that prepares people for life and helps them change for the better is precious for what it gives and the problems it resolves. Education makes us more aware, more flexible and less prejudiced. It helps us evolve in our thinking and our maturity. Learning something new everyday helps us to stay responsive and young in spirit. People become rigid with judgement. Judgement exhausts us and makes us older, but not wiser or more aware. As we learn our lessons, our life unfolds in its destined curriculum in the easiest and best possible manner, which builds our life for happiness. When we have failed a certain lesson, the pain of it stays with us, affecting that area and pulling down our life in general. But the lesson still awaits us and as we finally learn it the pain disappears, bringing a gift with a new level of confidence and awareness.

Life will knock louder and louder until we answer the door to learn the lesson. If we barricade the door or pretend no one is home, life has a way of knocking our door down to deliver the message. Further denial can lead to something catastrophic. There cannot be a problem unless we have hidden something from ourselves or deceived ourselves in some way. So the courage to learn what we have dissociated from ourselves heals us. These are not only painful but also often beautiful or transcendent experiences, which also threaten the ego. When we realise that our ego is a learning device and not the boss of our mind, unless we choose it to be, we will realise that we have more freedom to choose what we want. We will also learn that what threatens the ego does not necessarily threaten us.

Learning can be a very powerful factor for change in that we can learn something momentarily and change our world immediately. The further we go with our learning, the more we also begin to value unlearning as a healing principle. We see what is limiting or trapping us and we know there is something to be unlearned. At each point that we were able to pick up a dark lesson in our lives, we learned a mistaken lesson that we must unlearn to make us happy. Just the realisation that we made a mistake when we have unhappy times opens our minds to truly learn. When you have learned correctly then the pain and heaviness of the past will be released for current understanding and love. Unless you think you need the past to stay as it was for some current agenda, you will naturally be curious about how something that might have been so painful in the past could be just a mistake to be corrected. If you are invested in the past as an excuse now, your ego will feel threatened and you will get angry. While we only learn as fast as we want to learn, how fast we learn can dictate the quality of our lives. Motivation is the crucial factor in both learning and healing.

Exercise

It's time to examine the areas of your life to see how you're doing in specific learning situations.

1. First of all examine the size of your problem. Is it a tap on your door, or has your door been knocked down? The bigger the problem the bigger the hidden emotion, conflict and lesson.

2. Next examine your attitude toward learning because your attitude in each area becomes crucial.

- Are you heading toward success or suffering?
- Are you a resistant or happy learner?
- Do you attack yourself and say you can't learn something, belittling yourself and increasing your fears by your self-attack and negativity, which just hides your fear of going forward?
- Are you in a fight to learn a certain lesson, pretending it's just something to get through?

3. Examine some of the following areas regarding both your attitude and how well you are doing. Also, add some of your own categories that you consider important because of your life situation. Ask yourself the percentage to which you have learned this lesson. If you have learned the lesson and you are happy, successful and carefree in this area, your current learning is about one hundred percent.

Category	Attitude	How Well Am I Learning the Lesson?
• True Love		
• Relationships		
• Love in General		
• Abundance		
• Money		
• Leisure		

- Health
- Communication
- Emotions
- Openness
- Sex
- Career
- Purpose
- Confidence
- Success
- Family
- Parenting

If you are willing to let go of your control and agenda, there is an easy way for you to open and receive the lesson. Any part of your life that is problematic, where you have to have things your way or you are upset, is a place in which you have your ego's agenda going and lack confidence.

If you are courageous and willing to learn the lesson, there will be confidence and ease. Take any category and let go of your agenda around it. Ask heaven or your own higher mind to show you the way. As you let go of any past upset, fear, unwillingness to go forward, guilt, anger or other blocks, ask to receive the lesson which would free you, give you confidence and advance you.

Take one category and keep a journal about this area; this way you will notice when situations show themselves for learning. Everyday commit to learning easily in this area. Help and learning can also come from friends, school, books, co-workers, mentors, workshops, conferences, meetings, television, the

Internet, dreams or inspiration. Notice how your desire to learn and the willingness to give up your agenda frees you. *A Course In Miracles* suggests that we resign as our own teachers. Choose to learn the lesson. Want to learn the lesson. Be willing to learn the lesson. Notice how fast things can unfold after learning this lesson and how success can grow at a whole new level when you let go and ask to be shown the way.

Once this lesson feels complete – as proved not only by your freedom from the problem, but also by your empowerment – choose a new area that you would like furthered and follow this. How fast the situation comes to a new level of learning and success is how much your desire is greater than your fear.

WAY 2 Healing Fear

Fear is at the heart of every problem. One of the most effective ways to resolve a problem is to heal the fear within. What most people don't realise is that fear – like all emotions – begins with us. It comes from within us as a response. It is a result of our thinking and our way of looking at something. It is how we act and react that generates our fear.

Fear basically comes from separation. So any place we push away, such as in judgement, attack or withdrawal, we generate fear. We then project out what we are doing and see the world doing this to us. Our emotions are another example of how we reap what we sow. Though it is not true, we often believe that what is happening to us is caused by other people, or by some outside action. We believe ourselves to be passive, neutral observers. We believe that other people or situations make us feel something. Statements such as: 'He made me angry', 'She laid a guilt-trip on me' or 'He hurt me' are just a few examples. We simply don't realise how much our thoughts and responses generate our feelings. Wherever there is *no* love, bonding, understanding, joining or any of the healing principles which bring us together, there will be fear. It is the basis of all negative emotions. All emotions basically come down to two: love and fear, with fear being the illusion.

All fear comes from judgement and attack thoughts, directed toward the world around us. Fear does not have its origins outside us. As we think and act, so we see the world thinking and acting toward us. We project what we are doing and then experience ourselves feeling attacked and vulnerable, keeping us from sharing and joining with others. At this point we lose sight of the fact that the situation or feelings began as thoughts – thoughts that are at some level a choice and bring about self-fulfilling prophecies. Our thoughts literally build the world we see, heading us either towards life and happiness or towards suffering and death. As we become aware of the myriad of fear thoughts that come about as a result of judging others, the situation or ourselves, we can choose to give up these thoughts. One of the many ways to heal the fear at the root of every problem is to let go of our fear thoughts and negative beliefs, thereby opening us to a level of confidence, opportunity and giftedness, which quickly and easily resolves the outside situation.

To do this, we must first become aware of the thoughts that we have generated around a situation. Many of us are not even aware that we are having fear thoughts, which become self-fulfilling prophecies that run our lives. We go through our lives with these fear thoughts that we are consciously unaware of, and we have to become really frightened before we notice them. We do not realise how we attack ourselves by such thoughts. Our fears attract and bring our problems home to roost. They reinforce and subliminally call for that which we resist, bringing about the very thing that we are afraid would happen. Our fear weakens and paralyses us, keeping us from feeling confident or acting effectively. But our fear is bypassed whenever our desire for healing becomes stronger than our fear of the next step. Finally we are no longer held back by this feeling. No matter what the situation, our fear blocks our confidence and responsiveness.

Fear is trying to deal with the future before it arrives, which is impossible. The more we try to live in the future the more frightened we become, because we think our lives will be the same as whatever unresolved negativity there was in the past.

Fear comes from feelings of loss or separation. We will feel frightened to the extent that we feel cut off, abandoned, rejected and unwanted, with no one there to help us. Times in the past when we became isolated, separated or have lost bonding, which we have not healed, still exist inside us as fear. This means that unhappy memories from our past show themselves as fear or lack of confidence. But we can still only feel this fear now by thinking we're alone and that there is no one close to us, not even God. If we were to allow ourselves to feel the presence of God beside us, we would dissolve our fear the way light dissolves darkness. In the same way if we join with another, creating bonding in the here and now we will dissolve the fear. Many of us are carrying patterns of fear within us because of old pain locked inside. But after working with thousands of people who had major abandonment and rejection stories from childhood it soon became evident to me that there was much more going on than met the eye.

Anything that we have hidden from ourselves in darkness or anything that we have judged generates fear. Once we are willing to face what we have suppressed and repressed, what we have denied and dissociated, we can then begin to experience the buried emotions because we are no longer bullied by fear. We can finally begin to heal this experience. This problem could have been resolved if we had fully experienced – until it was gone – all of the initial feeling that was present when the pain first began. As we now get in touch with the subconscious elements of the mind, we begin to understand how much in the way of negative emotion we have hidden from ourselves. Whenever we bury emotions like this, it makes us more fearful. As we heal these emotions by feeling them through, coming to a new understanding, forgiveness or letting go, we grow in confidence and no longer see ourselves as unworthy. As a result of this healing, we no longer see ourselves as deserving of abandonment and rejection and a whole layer of self-attack falls away. Much of this occurs as we understand many of the hidden elements in our experience of abandonment, rejection and heartbreak. We begin to recognise ego strategies, hidden agendas and payoffs. We begin to realise that we have held the belief that paying a certain price in pain and negativity would allow us to achieve something that we thought would help or make us happy. This mistaken belief includes such dynamics as hiding and avoiding our purpose, having an excuse to attack someone, keeping or hiding an indulgence, demanding our way, wanting to be special, keeping a certain level of independence, attempting to defeat someone, desiring revenge and keeping fears of rejection and abandonment. These are an attempt to avoid even greater fears such as fear of relationship, intimacy, purpose, our true greatness or destiny. As we resolve the fears of abandonment and rejection, our relationship patterns take a giant step forward. In place of fear, withdrawal, dissociation, failure and trying too hard, we now feel confidence, loveableness, and irresistibility, as well as gifts of healing and strength.

Courage comes from the French word *coeur*, meaning 'heart'. The extent to which we have been and are broken-hearted, is the extent to which we will remain frightened. Fear will give rise to hurt, jealousy, insecurity, neediness, unwillingness, more heartbreak, dissociation, independence, lack of relationship, cynicism and bitterness. When we have lost heart through past experiences, our fear increases and we act in self-defeating ways. We then either withdraw or attack, hoping that someone will come to find us and save us with their love. We don't realise how self-defeating these behaviours are. If we are without a partner and we have not come into the world to be monks, nuns or follow a celibate path, then there is some major element of fear going on in spite of what we tell ourselves. Where there is scarcity in any area, we are afraid to receive, and thus we act in a self-defeating manner.

Confidence comes from the Latin word *con fides*, meaning 'with faith'. Confidence means we use our mind faithfully, building the situation and ourselves rather than attacking ourselves with fear thoughts or attacking others with judgement, which comes from fear, guilt and our need to see ourselves as being separate and superior to what we judge. If we attack or judge we will we see this same judgement coming back to us. This makes us fearful. When we are confident, however, we attack no one, not even ourselves. We cannot be upset because we will use the power of our minds to think and choose in a positive way, knowing that our experience will come back to us by how we choose and think. We neither sugarcoat our feelings nor the situation itself. We are not deceiving ourselves by wearing rose-tinted glasses, so we won't have a rude awakening when our denial is pierced. We just know that whatever is occurring does not have any ultimate power over us, because we have faith that the scene will unfold in the best possible way. Through the power of our mind, focused on the good, we are able to turn scenes that could have symbolised suffering, destruction or death into a means of attaining peace and success.

Our minds are powerful. They literally make up the world we see. Any attempt to diminish the power of our minds is a misguided effort to diminish our fears. This will only increase our fears in the long run because it replaces our ability and responsibility to change and improve our lives, making us dependent on chance or a fickle world that does not seem to have much regard for us.

One of the most common fears at the root of every problem is a fear of the next step. This comes from lack of confidence and fear of the unknown. Another key fear, which is a part of all fear, is the fear of loss, in which we see the next step as one in which we will lose something vital if we were to step forward. Fear comes from a conflict within, the result of having a split mind and wanting two different things. To move in either direction brings the fear to one side so that the other will lose. This can keep us in a dilemma, distracted, paralysed or delayed until it feels so intolerable that we repress the side of our mind we least identify with. This is the side which is projected out as the obstacle in our way. Fear also comes from power struggle. These conflicts outside us with another begin as conflicts within. Our split mind results in two different parts of our mind wanting and fighting for two different things, making us fearful. Only through resolution of the conflict and integration of both sides into a new whole, can we bring about a greater integrity that will focus us toward success without reservations or obstacles.

Finally, fear comes from our authority conflict, wanting to be the boss by attacking authority figures, leaders and God. This frightens us, because they seem to have more power. And if we see ourselves as betraying, we will fear betrayal. While resistance to anything generates fear, our resistance to authority and being told what to do, even if it is true, keeps us frightened. The extent to which we resist or attack authority figures is the extent of our fear of people in authority and how much we see God as a stern, judgmental figure rather than as a loving Father who only wants to help and bring about what is best for us.

If we were not so fearful about being told what to do, we would listen to the answers from within that would resolve our fear. We fight to be our own authority even when we are mistaken or failing. Not knowing what we really want, we identify with our egos and fight against ourselves. We are afraid to give up our way because we think we will lose our freedom as we lose our dissociated, reactive independence, not realising that we would experience much more freedom and truth in interdependence.

Fear comes from our thoughts and our beliefs. Beliefs are static, continuous thoughts which come about through the decisions we make, sometimes after painful ordeals. What we feel comes from what we think or believe. Fearful thoughts or beliefs lead to fearful emotions and frightening experiences which then reinforce our fearful beliefs.

Exercise

This exercise can take out the underpinning fear that holds a problem in place. It removes the key factor of self-attack incumbent in any fear. Make the choice to stop attacking yourself with negative thoughts.

At least five times today, for five minutes at a

time, reflect on a problem you wish to resolve. Be as specific as possible as you answer the following statement:

- In the situation regarding _____, what I am afraid will happen is _____.

Realise that each of these thoughts is a direct attack on yourself, eroding your confidence, your safety, and your success.

- This thought is generating my problem and is keeping me from moving forward.
- Do I want to keep doing this to myself?

You will notice that after five or six times of doing this five-minute exercise some very significant fear or self-attack thoughts will surface. At the end of each practice period say: 'I don't want to keep attacking myself like this. What I choose to think now is _____.'

WAY 3 Be Attitudes or Bad Attitudes

Our attitude comes from the continual choices we make. Choice after choice made in the same direction becomes our attitude, either positively or otherwise. Our attitude is probably the most important choice we make in life because there are only two directions we can take. We either have a *be* attitude of blessing, giving and enjoying the world around, which is where we give out our fullness and wholeness, or we have a *bad* attitude that has its own 'taking' agenda. There is something we are trying to get when we have a negative attitude and we get angry if someone seems to get in our way. Our bad attitude can take the form of righteousness, power struggle, indulgence, suffering or death. A be attitude values healing, learning, happiness, love and life. In some areas we may be aiming toward life while in other areas we choose to move toward death. We may not even be aware of which direction we are moving in until we examine it, but once we do, it's typically a simple choice. I have sometimes asked people who have major problems or catastrophic illness to measure where they are on this life scale:

Life Attitude Scale

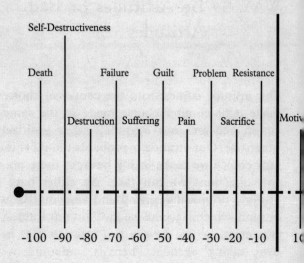

Self-Destructiveness

Death   Failure   Guilt   Problem Resistance

Destruction Suffering   Pain   Sacrifice   Motiv

-100 -90 -80 -70 -60 -50 -40 -30 -20 -10   10

If they find that they are on the negative side of the scale, they can simply choose to turn around and move into the positive range toward life. Of course we are all so good at self-deception, projection, hiding, compensating, denying and repressing our conflicts, revenge, rebellion and general bad attitude, that many times we don't realise we actually have a bad attitude, such as when we perceive something as another's problem or fault rather than as part of our responsibility by being in the situation. Being a victim reflects a hidden or not so hidden bad attitude. Sometimes we find ourselves peeling back layer after layer of this bad attitude we never realised we possessed. The effectiveness of responsibility is that its innocence makes it responsive, co-operative and helpful rather than judgmental, superior and acquisitive.

Accidents, illnesses or chronic problems that are trapping us and generating pain demonstrate common symptoms of bad attitudes we have hidden from ourselves. This means, among other things, that we are going in the wrong direction and that we have some goal or hidden agenda that is taking us away from life toward death. When we discover this within ourselves it is crucial to make another choice. We can choose to be open, willing and amenable to the guidance within. We can also choose to desire the truth, correct our mistakes, learn the lessons and ask for help while unlearning dark, painful lessons. We can make new and positive decisions, pour our trust into a positive outcome, let go of attachments, indulgences, dark beliefs, guilt and death temptations.

While allowing ourselves to forgive ourselves and others, we can give up separation, judgement and join with others, commit to life, our partner and our gifts, live our purpose, embrace our destiny and ask for a miracle. All these healing principles turn us towards a life direction which builds our lives.

All the choices we make that either head toward life or head away from death, create healing. There are no neutral spots; we are either heading toward life or heading toward death and all the time we are able to choose. Whatever is a trap, obsession or an obstacle to our peace is not only a problem in and of itself, but it is also a sign of sin, destruction and death to us. By our attitude we can choose to see the very thing we use to decide for a negative direction, as that which becomes the means for healing and peace. When we do this we are turning in a positive direction and our problems become learning and healing situations – the very stuff of positive attitudes.

Exercise

Beware that the ego tries to stop your awareness by blaming yourself. It uses guilt to halt you from discovering what is under your denial. Promise not to fall for this. Whenever you experience guilt, turn it over to your higher mind for resolution. Your willingness to have guilt undone will dissolve it and its accompanying fear for you. Know it is not the truth, which is why all guilt can be resolved and turned into responsibility, learned lessons and maturity.

Otherwise we will use the guilt we all have inside of us as a form of unwillingness that keeps us separate and turned toward death. Don't turn toward a direction that you wouldn't want someone you love to also turn toward.

Measure yourself on the Life Attitude Scale. If you are on the positive side, choose to become more positive. Examine different aspects of your life in this way.

If you are on the negative side, make a new choice and imagine yourself turning around and coming up into the positive side of the scale. Make the choice to use anything negative in your life as a means of learning, healing, peace and happiness.

If you have a problem that is upsetting you, recognise that there is a hidden negative attitude and make the choice to discover it, while wanting truth, healing, peace and life.

Examine the word which best applies to you as an indication of what is going on in areas such as love and relationships, sex, money, creativity, work, success, happiness, health and ease. Recognise that wherever you are on the chart is what you want and are giving in the situation. If you give only the positive, then the positive is what you will reap. Commit to find what you have hidden from yourself so you can choose again. You can change your mind now for yourself and those you love.

WAY 4   Understanding

A problem is the result of a misunderstanding, some kind of ego illusion. If we understood our situation fully, the problem would resolve itself. I have found understanding to be a crucial and primordial element not only in releasing people from problems, but also in restoring bonding and innocence lost through separation and misunderstanding. The deeper the understanding, the greater the release of fear, need, grievance and loss, all of which are core aspects of any problem. When traced back, both the emotional pain that comes from problems and the problems themselves, are ultimately based on misunderstandings which generate separation and lead to judgement. Judgement then increases the misunderstanding and separation, which also increases the guilt. Judgement and/or sacrifice is then used to hide the guilt. Without understanding we live in a landscape of illusion, without bonding, ease, intimacy or success. We are stuck in a pattern that hides fear, guilt and feelings of loss. Such a pattern instils unwillingness and reinforces future illusion and misunderstandings.

Years ago, when working in drug rehabilitation, I realised that problems could be solved and pain could be dissolved because they actually weren't true. When a mistaken perception was corrected or when a profound understanding came about, so did a profound healing. These healings through understanding were far beyond mere intellectual ideas and significantly transformed the situations involved. Problems can be built one upon another in layers, with the top ones defending much bigger problems beneath them. Where we have understanding, and thus trust, we do not stop, but continue moving through layer after layer until a particular pattern is healed and complete, and peace and joy are there as a result.

The following exercise allows us to move through layer after layer until we reach peace and resolution. In this we usually move from shallower to deeper areas of the mind and many times continue into the levels of the superconscious, as evidenced by the joy which becomes present. This easy, helpful method is called the 5 *Why* method and was developed by Jeremy Roe to get to the hidden cause of things. When I realised this could be adapted as a healing method, I merely extended the method by repeating it until the client reached beyond the problem to a state of joy. The power of repeating the *why's* allows us to move through and let go of each of the layers present. As we move to a deeper understanding of *why*, the previous level, which is shallower, falls away. Even if the same answer is repeated on a subsequent level, it will now have a greater depth than when it was the response for the previous *why*. By using this process, people have reported feeling they had saved themselves years' worth of work, problems and suffering. As we move through each successive layer especially the heavier ones, we begin to feel lighter and lighter, and naturally move up into the spiritual and joyful parts of our mind if we wish to go that far.

Exercise

You can do this exercise with a pen and paper, a tape recorder or a friend.

1. Ask yourself (if you are doing it with a friend, have your friend ask you) why do I (you) have this problem? Reply with the first thing that comes into your mind. Repeat the question and write down, or record on tape, each response until you have asked and responded five times. This fifth response now becomes the 'why' for the next cycle.

    The following are examples:

- *Why do I have this illness? I'm sick to death.*
- *Why do I have this illness? I'm so tired.*
- *Why do I have this illness? I need a break.*
- *Why do I have this illness? I'm so bored.*
- *Why do I have this illness? I'm stuck.*

    Use the fifth response to begin a new cycle:

- *Why am I stuck? I don't know the way.*
- *Why am I stuck? I'm afraid to find the way.*
- *Why am I stuck? I don't want to find the way.*
- *Why am I stuck? I'd hate to find the way.*

• *Why am I stuck? I don't want to give my parents the satisfaction of knowing I found the way.*

Then start a new cycle of *why's* using the fifth response of this previous cycle.

• *Why don't I want to give my parents the satisfaction of knowing I found the way? Etc.*

Continue the exercise until you feel happy and complete.

2. Alternatively, you could just ask and pray for the understanding that would resolve and release the problem. Understanding means you see the process involved and how to move through it easily.

WAY 5   The Call to Change

Every problem is a fear of and a refusal to change. Problems are wake up calls and crucial lessons to let us know that how we are will not sustain us. Things are not yet complete, a greater success is ahead and it is important not to delay here. It is time to let go of whatever the attachment is that has been holding us back and keeping us from change so we can journey on in a more successful way. We are called upon to be courageous and to take new steps. The experience of a loss in our lives is especially a call for a new birth. It lets us know that what we had been relying on is not really our answer and more is called for. It reminds us to trust more in our own higher power, which will help and sustain us, than in something or someone outside ourselves. This problem reminds us that it is now time to let go of something outside of us and recognise the power back within ourselves.

Our change is our cure. If we stay where we are, unchanging and separate, then we begin to turn in a death direction. If we keep doing what we have been doing, we'll just have more of what we already have. Transformation is called upon. The problem signifies that we can't get there from here. The only solution is to change. Our *willingness* to change allows change to occur within us and unfold around us. Our willingness to change says Yes! to life. It accepts the situation, allowing it to transform and take us to a new level. Today our willingness will cut through our fear and attachment, naturally and easily changing us. The size of the problem reflects the size of the shift being offered to us. We are called to have courage and confidence for a better way of life.

Exercise

Imagine you are at a crossroads. One of the choices facing you will take you forward in a whole new, but true, direction. The other choice eventually circles back until you will be at the same crossroads once again a few years from now. Take the new way you are called upon to be a leader. When you do say Yes! to this new direction, Yes! to life and Yes! to your higher mind, you may experience a period of disruption. It is important to remember that this is just the birth process which is needed to complete the change. Don't stop here; trust the process and you will continue moving through any disquiet until you've reached a new plateau in your life.

WAY 6 Healing Guilt

In every problem guilt is a key dynamic. Guilt is one of the ego's most destructive strategies. The ego is built on and anchored by self-attack and with-drawal. Guilt believes in grandiosity, dark glamour and self-punishment rather than in correcting mis-takes. Guilt constantly reinforces the mistake and keeps us stuck into never learning the lesson. The ego's purpose with guilt is to keep us from moving forward by using fear of the next step and fear of intimacy. While guilt is feeling bad about the past, we use it to punish ourselves in order to hold onto the past in a vain attempt to get needs met now that were unmet then. This of course cannot work. These hidden needs can only be met in the present through forgiveness, joining and giving-receiving. These healing responses call for an end to the withdrawal brought about by guilt, which at one level still waits for someone to come and save us with their love, telling us we were innocent. Healing returns us to the contact and connection that leads to success. It brings back our innocence and allows us to learn the lesson through a new level of understanding.

Guilt manifests in symptoms such as unrewarded hard work, sacrifice and roles (forms of doing without giving ourselves). It also shows up as self-attack, failure, illness, defeat, depression, righteousness, unworthiness, difficulty, valuelessness, compensation, judgement, attack from others or attack on others. *A Course in Miracles* says that we never crucify ourselves alone. With guilt we not only punish ourselves, but we also crucify those around us whom we love. By our behaviour we teach and reinforce the same behaviour in the world. Guilt is adamant in its stubbornness, refusing to learn its lesson and go forward, thus keeping this area of our lives arrested and unsuccessful.

At times guilt is part of a competition for specialness by being the best of the worst. At other times, guilt is an attempt to get approval. For example, we may have done a bad thing but now feel appropriately guilty and remorseful to prove we can't be all that bad. We attempt to have others meet our needs by punishing us or feeling bad for us, but this further separates us from them. Most of the guilt that rules us, causing us to live our lives in compensation of unrewarded hard work and sacrifice, was already present in childhood. This guilt also shows itself symptomatically as anger, dissociation, sacrifice, fusion (losing the natural boundaries between others and ourselves) and self-defeating patterns. It is the quintessential form of delay.

While we all feel guilty, it is important to commit to freeing others and ourselves from guilt. Most people use guilt to control themselves and others in an effort to prevent the same mistake happening again, but guilt actually reinforces the mistake. With guilt we either continue in the pattern of the mistake, because our guilt gives negative attention and is a major reinforcer, which causes more guilt, or we have to withdraw from the situation further for fear of repeating what made us feel guilty. Some people use guilt to allow themselves to keep doing something 'bad' they wish to continue doing, if only they pay the price of feeling guilty about it afterwards.

Guilt then is a form of self-punishment with secondary payoffs of not having to face our next step of intimacy and purpose. *A Course in Miracles* states that guilt is a form of arrogance because we decide in favour of our egos, which declares us guilty and against God who declares us innocent.

Exercise

To get beyond the ego and its resistance, it is important to trust your intuition in all of the exercises. Ask yourself the following question until you have the answer you know is true:

- *By having this problem I am punishing myself because I feel I failed with _____.*

Reflect on your willingness to let go of the past and to have it be corrected by your higher mind. Make the following declaration of your freedom at least three times a day – in the morning, afternoon and night, or as often as needed until you return to feeling good:

I will no longer use these problems as self-punishment to hold myself back. I choose to forgive myself so that I may learn the lesson and move forward.

WAY 7 Forgiveness

Every problem we experience comes as the result of an attack, grievance or judgement against another. It can be the biggest or smallest of problems, but our judgement and attack keep us caught in problems and the situation we have judged. Like many attack thoughts, we think of them in a split second and then immediately bury them. However, these attack thoughts also attack us, locking us into the situation we have judged. Our judgements come out of our own guilt, which is typically more hidden.

Innocence, on the other hand, does not blame or attack. It recognises only love or the call for love. Forgiveness resolves the hidden guilt and withdrawal that keeps us from moving forward and succeeding. Forgiveness allows us to give forth to others. It removes the judgement on ourselves, which was projected onto others, and changes our perception of both them and us. Forgiveness frees everyone. As our perception changes, the other's does as well and the situation changes. Forgiveness actually transforms and releases us from the situation in which we were in pain and sacrifice and allows us to see that it was just a misunderstanding. We can now respond to the behaviour of others as a call for help. Forgiveness restores the bonding and ends the separation and as a result it leads us closer to the joyful consciousness of unity. Forgiveness heals a conflict within us as it brings peace and happiness to a conflict outside us. Forgiveness is the heart of all the healing principles, ending the withdrawal that every grievance and judgement brings about. There is no situation that forgiveness cannot resolve.

Exercise

If you were walking down the pavement and a little child came up to you in tears, would you push him away or kick him out into the street? Imagine the person you have a grievance with is standing right in front of you. This time do not limit your assessment of this person to just how they are acting, but look inside them. See the wounded child, or children, within them which cause them to act the way they do. Would you kick them away? Would you refuse to help them? You couldn't be in such a situation if there was not a wounded child within you as well. How old is the wounded child, or children, inside of you? Are you willing to help both the other and yourself? If you are, let the wounded child in you go to the wounded child in them. Through holding them and loving them all the wounded children will heal and grow up. When they reach your present age, yours will melt into you and theirs will melt into them, bringing new life, love and success, with ease and energy.

WAY 8 Purpose

When I had been conducting therapy for about ten years, I began to see something I had not noticed before. Once resolved, the problems my clients were dealing with seemed to be for the most part distractions, delays and deceptions. I became curious about what these problems were hiding, and soon it became clear that most people's problems were a way of avoiding their purpose in life. This avoidance both trivialised their lives and took away their sense of direction. I began to see that about 85 percent of all of our problems are set up unconsciously as part of this conspiracy against ourselves – a conspiracy against our purpose and greatness. I found that when we find our sense of purpose, most of our problems seem to fall away naturally and whatever problems remain are necessary to bring about the learning experiences for our purpose.

Love and purpose fill our lives with meaning. Our purpose is an act of love from us to the world. We all share a number of life purposes such as love and happiness. When we are not in a state of love and happiness, then we share the purpose of healing ourselves to recover these states of joy. Also, we are all called upon to help the world and save it from its suffering. For most of us this means healing and transforming the situations we are in. This has an automatic and ever widening positive ripple effect throughout the world.

Then there is the purpose which is personal to each of us. It is our promise to give to the world in a certain way. It is our calling and that which we, of all the people in the world, are best suited to do. It is a unique combination of who we are and what we are inspired to do. *A Course In Miracles* states that if we do not answer this personal call, it remains unanswered.

Our purpose fulfils us. It is our vocation, which both thrills and frightens us until we allow ourselves to remember and embrace it. It is our function that is both unique and special to us. Our purpose can grow and change with time so that we typically have a number of purposes throughout our lives. To know our purpose gives us a clear direction in which to head. It is a movement toward life rather than death. It is what we can do to make our life more happy and fulfilled. It is what we can do to help others and ourselves. Our ego in an attempt to stop us tells us that we have a big purpose, but that we could not possibly accomplish it. It tries to frighten us, telling us it's impossible and we are too small to do something so great. Yes, our purpose is typically more than we think we can accomplish, but we will not do it so much as it will be done through us by grace. Our job is to show up and be willing to let what is inspired be done through us. What is too big for us to handle is nothing for heaven. It is time to step up into all we are and contribute all we have come to give.

Exercise

Today you are asked to focus on what it is you would really love to do, but might be frightened to begin.

- What was it you promised at a soul level?
- What would you love to do?
- What calls you?
- What could you give that truly inspires you, yet feels too big or frightening?
- If you had a magic wand and could give anything you wanted to the world, what would it be?

You don't have a magic wand but you do have a great heart and mind along with friends in high places.

Choose your purpose. Choose to leap to this new way of living. This may mean that you will go through disruption, as your life is rearranged from getting to giving so that you can live your purpose. But now is the time to keep faith until you have reached a newer, happier level and are more truly living your purpose.

- Choose your purpose.
- Commit to your true life path.
- Want your purpose with all your heart.
- Be willing to show up to do what you are inspired to do and receive the help and grace to accomplish your purpose.

WAY 9   Letting Go

Every problem we have reflects a certain attachment, hidden or otherwise, that is holding onto someone or something from the past. This attachment is the main outcome we would like to have happen again, even if it goes against reality. An attachment can also be an indulgence or addiction which is meant to make up for the past. In meeting the goal of an attachment that is based on fantasy, we think a certain need of ours would finally be met. Needs, which are attachments, always have a certain psychological urgency accompanying them, but this very urgency blocks receiving. The more we need something the more resistance we create around receiving it. We try to take from others whatever we think we need, which sets up resistance on the giver's part. Our need subtly pushes the giver and the giving away. Every need is counterproductive to its own desire. Frustration and disappointments, which always accompany attachments, needs and the expectations they set up, teach us that the source of happiness is not outside but within.

Every need in the present actually represents an old need that was never met in the past. It is impossible to get a past need met in a present situation, since the past doesn't exist anymore. It is vain and frustrating to try to rectify pain and loss from the past. Only disappointment can come from such effort. There is a subconscious dynamic that says we can't lose anything we fully want or value, so whatever seems to have been lost from the past wasn't fully valued. Somehow our loss occurred as the result of a split mind on our part. We are attempting to use something that didn't satisfy us in the past to try to satisfy ourselves now.

When we hold on, we hold onto a fantasy. To fantasise about a picture of what will meet our need means that our hands are not open to receive because when the receiver is ready, the giver appears and fantasy isn't necessary. This means when we are holding on to some old picture, we are actually afraid to receive. The paradox with holding on is that we can never have or keep that to which we are attached.

Letting go is a paradox that opens us to receive something we prefer but don't need. Letting go is not throwing something away, nor is it dissociating which is actually a secret attempt to gain control by not getting hurt. Dissociation is actually a sign that a lot is still being held onto. Letting go is, rather, a detachment that puts everything back in perspective and brings the source of our happiness from outside ourselves back to within us. This allows flow and development in the situation and a true relationship with others that moves us forward. Letting go brings attractiveness, peace, a feeling of balance and opens us to receive.

Another form of our attachment is an indulgence, which is an attempt to make up for some past need or pain and to relieve us from the exhaustion of

sacrifice. Whether emotional or physical, an indulgence shows a high level of attachment which can
turn into tantrums or addictions. Often we hide
these indulgences, at least from ourselves, because
of shame or guilt and they become that much harder
to find and heal. Many times hidden under a chronic
problem that will not resolve is a hidden indulgence
we are so attached to we refuse to let go. The chronic
problem is both the cover and the compensation for
the indulgence. We know that if we took the next
step we would lose the indulgence we are using to
medicate ourselves. An indulgence can never make
us happy, as it is a form of separation and fantasy
all mixed together.

Exercise

Today, identify your need and attachment in a
present problem situation. Somehow it is your
holding on which is not allowing the situation to
move forward. Once you have identified your need,
ask yourself:

- *If I were to know when this need I am trying to
  satisfy now began, it was when _____.*
- *If I were to know who it was with, it was probably with _____.*
- *If I were to know what occurred, it was probably
  _____.*

Let go of this scene and all of the needs, feelings
and beliefs which came about. Be willing to let the

feelings and the needs go so that you can move forward and succeed. It takes courage to be empty-handed, but it is one of the easiest ways to move forward. Letting go is simply a statement that you will no longer try to get in the present what you thought you wanted from the past. It is a willingness to recognise that what you wanted from outside you probably wasn't there to get. It was and is inside you and ready to be shared. If this choice to let go is made then nothing else is necessary.

Here are three other ways of letting go which are different but effective. Use one or all of them in your present circumstance. There are two primary, but opposite forms of letting go. One is for you to feel, even exaggerate, the hidden pain and sadness under your need until they finally become positive feelings. The other is to put your attachment and the past in the hands of God. When you give up something that is illusory and painful, it not only frees you, it is also a gift to God, the world and those you love. See or feel what God gives back to you as a result of your giving him the attachment.

Become willing to let go of any chronic problem and the indulgence which hides underneath it. When you realise it is counterfeit and that it is stopping you from what would really make you happy, you are ready. Imagine that you put your indulgence on a rocket going to the farthest reaches of outer space. Then shoot off the rocket. If this uncovers old pain and need, then put it on another rocket into outer space. When all this is gone, open yourself to the next step forward.

WAY 10 The Power of Choice

A problem reflects a choice we made for some reason and immediately repressed, a choice which was designed to get something. Our choice led to the problem. There was something we thought this choice would give us, which would make us happy. That the choice we made was a mistake is evident in the problem and the trouble, and the unhappiness it is bringing us. Whatever reason we had for choosing this problem, it was a mistake and it can be corrected the same way it began – by choice. For example, we cannot have a problem or be feeling poorly unless we have chosen to judge someone. We can *choose* to let this judgement go and regain our happiness.

Understanding the choice we made and why we made it goes a long way in helping us make another choice. That we immediately repressed our choice makes it at once suspect. We surely wouldn't bury anything that we weren't afraid to look at. In our lives we have forgotten more than we remember but all the billions of choices we have made and the experiences we have had are all in our mind. If they are negative they generate experiences and will need to be undone.

The first step in undoing a current problem is the recognition that it is the result of a mistaken choice and that we no longer want it. At this point we can make another choice. The second step is to be willing to be wrong about the situation because if we are right, we will be stuck with the way things are. If we are wrong about it, we allow ourselves to perceive it differently and to learn a truer way. Just to acknowledge a mistake on our part allows our mind to begin to look for a better way. We can make a better choice for what we want, thus opening a new way. Just as we chose a way which caused the problem, we can choose to resolve it. Remember, we must be sure to choose in such a way in which no one has to lose so as not to find ourselves caught in another problematic situation.

Although we can make choices at any time, the mind is most receptive to effective choosing just before going to sleep and just after waking up because our higher mind is fully alert at this point. For the most part, our world is a result of our unrecognised choices. Now we have a chance to reflect and choose what we want. A choice for a negative situation is typically made and repressed in a split second, leaving no visible sign of the choice except for the ensuing problem. We can ask ourselves when we made the choice for a certain problem and for what reason. Then we can imagine ourselves back there re-choosing in a more enlightened way.

Even if our problem seems like it's someone else's fault, it is the result of a mistaken choice on our part, some kind of ego plan. The ego will then give us a solution which will not work and will make no sense except to the ego, which will want to see the mistakes in others and have them change while denying our own mistakes. This will lead to a limited solution because how we see and treat them is how we will see and treat ourselves, which will cause a problem situation later. This will lead to endless repair and no solution. If we would be willing to listen to our higher mind it will supply a solution which will be a lesson in sharing and will work.

Exercise

1. Today, choose what you want instead of the problem. Make sure it's a solution where everyone wins and there's only acceptance and no judgement on anyone or you will choose an answer which won't last. How you see everyone in the situation will be how you treat yourself consciously or subconsciously, and a solution with judgement isn't a solution.

- See, feel and hear what you want. Then imagine sending your new choice out into the universe. Your response will arrive back to you as soon as you have confidence to have the answer.
- See, feel and hear how happy you will be when it comes. Things happen almost magically when we use our power of choice. Every time the thought of a certain problem crosses your mind, let it go and make a new choice. If a problem seems chronic, employ the steps suggested on the preceding page. Every time you

think of your problem, make a new choice for
what you want. Each choice can clear a layer
of the problem if not the problem itself.

2. Take responsibility for what has occurred so
far. This re-establishes your power to choose.
Turn your present judgements of everyone and
their mistakes in this problem situation over to
your higher mind. Now turn over all of your
mistakes and judgements on yourself over to
your higher mind. Anytime you are trying to
correct someone, it will come from your ego
judging their ego and you won't find a solution. Ask your higher mind for a solution which
includes sharing, truth and success for
everyone. Don't settle for anything less than
total success or you will have to redo things
and try again soon enough. Only heaven or
your higher mind can do this.

WAY 11   The Call to Leadership

Any problem avoids the calls for help that surround us. A problem is also a distraction and a form of self-attack, which deafens us to those who need us. Responding to the calls for help is the essence of Leadership. Problems make us self-conscious, they shrink, obsess and trap us in an attempt to stop us being aware of others' needs. After a year and a half of searching for the root issue of the problems of shyness, self-consciousness, self-attack, self-torture, embarrassment, shame and humiliation, I was surprised to find that the key dynamic involved was a self-obsession that was an attempt to distract us from someone in need of help. As a result of our self-attack and shrinking, we didn't hear the call for help around us. One of the things I found about pain is that when we have a problem, there is someone else who is in even greater need who requires our help. Leadership is the art of responsiveness. If we respond to the call for help, both we and those who need us are helped. Responsiveness creates flow for us and for everyone involved. With this flow we are both moved forward out of the self-absorption which halts our progress and at least a layer of the problem. The purpose of any problem, which is an ego plan, is to restrain our personal growth and joy, which melts the ego, layer by layer.

Leadership is the desire to help. *A Course In Miracles* states that if we want to help we will hear the calls for help. Leadership and its incumbent responsiveness is one of the easiest ways to heal a problem, or at least a layer of the problem. Sometimes a big problem with many layers indicates that we may be called to help many people individually or to begin a project, which would help many people. Leadership allows for luck and opportunity; it opens the door to intuition and inspiration. Leadership makes the one in need of help more important than our pain or problem, not by some avoidance of our problem, but in the realisation that as we help, so are we helped. In our choice to overcome all obstacles out of our desire to help another, we willingly step through our pain, problem or any narcissistic self-involvement to reach them, and in stepping past the limitations imposed by the problem we are also freed.

Leadership is one of the easiest of the transformative methods I've found. It is effective in both large and small problems. There is no problem which does not respond effectively to our answering a call for help. Every time we join someone part of the ego melts away and we are both released. People need us and it is much truer to reach out to them than fret or worry about ourselves through self-attack or self-consciousness. This is a way to make the other's cry for help more important, and in so doing, free ourselves in responsiveness to others.

Exercise

Imagine the whole purpose of your problem has been your ego's desire to keep you separate, so you don't hear the calls for help around you. Decide that helping whoever you are called to help, is more important than worrying or obsessing about your problem. Ask yourself:

- *Who needs my support and help now?*

Call, write, visit or send love to whoever jumps into your mind. If these approaches do not seem appropriate, ask yourself intuitively how to proceed. Imagine that as you hear their call for help, you also step through the wall the problem has built around you, and that as you step through the problem falls away. If it is a big problem, sometimes only a layer of it falls away. If so, repeat this exercise as often and as best you can to remove even more layers until the whole problem falls away.

WAY 12 Vision

Unless we are living a joyful, loving and creative adventure in life, we are living one programmed by the past and what it lacked. Vision, on the other hand, is a state in which the positive future directs the present moment. Vision, a transpersonal state which transfigures perception, shows the way forward and brings success and creative energy into the present. Perception is dictated by unresolved past events that are now the filter through which and by which we see. This unfinished business leaves us feeling unrequited and unfulfilled and this is how we experience our present. As the unfinished business manifests itself now, it demands that someone sacrifice to make up for the past. Sacrifice means we are doing for others, but not truly giving ourselves or letting ourselves receive for what we do. When we give ourselves completely, situations automatically open to greater possibilities. Thus, vision transcends perception and brings the energy of heightened awareness, which accomplishes even the seemingly impossible both easily and creatively, without the need for anyone to lose or sacrifice themselves.

Vision is more of an act of receiving than giving, though it can at times be invited by wholehearted giving. It is essentially an act of love, which allows us to see the way through trying and even dangerous situations and obviates most of the difficulties present in them. Most of our traps, as they are generated by guilt and fear, are attempts to block vision. Vision not only creates a win for us, but also for those around us. Vision, which is both life enhancing and generative, allows for a truer, more successful way of living, bringing the progressive and transformative energy of the future into the present situation. While the experience of vision may be a solitary event, it affects and effects every area of our personal, social or life focus. Vision is a profound joining of heart and mind. As such, it is transformative, with creative, clear direction. By completely giving and venturing ourselves, we put everything on the line and open ourselves to greater awareness, especially of the successful pathways to the future. The love, energy and art of vision step across the abyss to the future and build a bridge for others to follow. Vision takes what looks like a death or failure situation and shows it clearly as an opportunity for birth, because at its heart vision is really an act of surrender and receiving of the creative force. By giving ourselves totally, or by being open and withholding nothing, we manage to resolve old fractures of the mind so that in their integration there is a birth of vision, which is naturally shared.

In spite of how we perceive it, any problem we are experiencing is an attempt to try to *get* something. This directs and determines our perception of the situation and locks us into self-defeating, aggressive or defensive responses. We are then blind to vision which would free and open us to greater possibilities and the way through, but can only be brought about by courageous receiving and magnanimous giving. Paradoxically vision is a way of receiving at an utmost, exquisite and abundant level though it cannot come about through any attempt to *take* or *get*.

There are three levels of vision, each one being more energetically powerful and creative. The higher the vision the stronger the ecstasy, though this is a by-product and vision cannot be achieved by trying to 'get' ecstasy. Ecstasy comes from the Latin *ex stasis*, meaning standing out of or out from, and it fits the experience because we stand out of our bodies in vision more and more. Vision is always a leap in consciousness, power and creativity.

The first level of vision is human vision. This is artistic vision where we give ourselves so fully to a certain thing we reach an altered state where we lose self-consciousness and reach a heightened awareness. We stop doing and it starts doing us. Whether it is painting, work, dancing, sport or love-making, we are carried away by its essence and force. Psychic gifts, which we all have to some degree, show up on all three levels of vision with an ever greater power. Vision is a theta brain-wave state which at times experiences synasthesia, which is a mixing of the senses. For instance, in the experience of synasthesia you could feel or see music not just metaphorically but literally, or what you see could have its own sound or smell. The positive future and the way through can show itself from all three levels if that is the focus of the vision.

The second stage of vision is the shamanic. This is where there is a transcendence of the natural laws governing time and space. By moving past consensual reality to a more ancient, original metaphoric reality, healings can be accomplished, prophecies made and the way through current problems found.

The third stage of vision is spiritual vision. This is where the polarity of perception is transcended so there's only the experience of unity, the interconnection of all things. There are experiences of light and a looking to spiritual reality, correcting the illusion and suffering of consensual everyday reality. Here there are experiences of the Great Rays, heaven, God, oneness, spiritual knowledge which comes from the eternal, revelation and the deepest experiences of love and joy.

With any vision we have the ability to save a great deal of time focusing more and more on what's important. Vision moves like a rocket, in that we are going fast and far and many times reaching places we couldn't otherwise reach. At the same time we're letting go of stages of the rocket that helped us get where we are but are no longer essential.

Exercise

To achieve vision you must uncover what you are passionate about.

- What would you love to do?

- Where would you feel you are totally giving your heart?
- What is it you want to leave behind after your death?
- What would you like your legacy for the world to be?
- What would you be thrilled to do?
- What adventure would call you to venture yourself fully?
- If you had a magic wand, what is the main thing which you would give to this world?

By letting go of judgement and continuously giving yourself for a couple of weeks or months to everyone and everything around you, you can achieve a state of vision. When you give yourself without reservation, soul wounds can heal and a birth of vision and visionary gifts comes about.

When the world opens to you and your heart is deeply filled with love, transcendence and the creative force, then you know you are experiencing vision.

Vision comes from focusing your awareness so fully outside yourself that you are no longer self-conscious, self-obsessed, or self-contained. This concentration outside yourself opens you to enhanced awareness and connection, allowing you to receive the creative force of vision and to see the greater possibilities that had previously been hidden from you.

Vision can be achieved through fasting, retreat and intention as in vision quests. It is also sometimes brought about through the deepest levels of communication with another or a single intuitive leap.

Vision can be received through your wholehearted desire to receive it, because anything which is wholly desired is accomplished with ease. A prayer or request to heaven or your higher mind can then bring it about through your openness and desire. Vision is a great gift to us and the world.

WAY 13 Getting Over Conflict

Many times we think we want two different and sometimes opposite things. A split mind causes us to go in different directions which means we end up nowhere. We want to stay true to whatever dream or path we are following, but we have curiosity, idle wishes, temptations and fear that we might lose something along the way. We have felt great need, fear, loss, depression, pain, desire, guilt, unworthiness and inadequacy. Rather than deal with the split mind which these feelings represent, we further cover it over by compensating for these feelings and acting the opposite way. Actions, which are compensations, include such behaviours as acting opposite to how we feel, attacking, dissociating from feeling, pretending something wasn't real, being busy or lazy, acting out roles, working too hard, refusing to receive, driving ourselves, being a perfectionist, punishing ourselves, acting superior or inferior, projecting the pain or problem outside ourselves, refusing help, demanding, attacking ourselves, refusing to relax, taking everything on our shoulders, having difficulty and making things hard on ourselves only to sabotage it. All these reflect the conflict within, though the compensation is an attempt to smooth things over and hide it.

Conflicts show themselves in many ways. Any sort

of judgement is the subconscious reflection of one part of our mind judging another part of our mind. Any imbalance in our lives speaks of an imbalance in our mind. Any conflict with anyone or anything outside us demonstrates a conflict within us. Similarly, any scarcity or lack in our lives conveys to us that there is some hidden opposition to abundance on our part, and it shows that we have made an investment in something other than abundance. Illness, injury or an accident denotes a place of hidden agenda or ego in our mind different than our conscious intention. Problems indicate a conflict; an aspect of the mind in which the side less identified with is experienced outside us as obstruction. Shadow figures or people outside ourselves that we hate or can't stand denote places of unconscious judgement and self-hatred within us. Any upset, problem or bad feeling represents a grievance and something we haven't forgiven in someone, which similarly reflects a judgement against ourselves. All of these aspects along with defences denote a conflict within us.

For the most part the experience of conflict is the experience of pain. It can get so painful that we want to die even if the conflict is not conscious. When death is not a peaceful leaving of our body, as easy as when we step out of our clothes, it represents a conflict we couldn't resolve. When we can't stand where we are and don't want to change, we are in a conflict so big we begin to turn in a direction of death. Where we are stuck in our lives is where we are stuck in conflict, and when that occurs in a significant way we begin to turn away from life. Illness represents a place where we are stuck: a place we believe we've sinned, a place of conflict and tantrum, a place we are fighting to be right, projecting our wrongs on someone else as a grievance. We all experience ourselves as conflicted and while it is not our true nature, it is the present state of humanity. We need only look out at the world to find evidence for this. Deep within our mind there remains a state of wholeness, of deepest peace and holiness, which few people get to experience given the present state of personal and collective evolution. This deepest part of ourselves is a state of oneness that is within us as the most essential or eternal part of us. It is what our souls are evolving toward and is the recognition of ourselves as spirit. This is a place of will, power, love, light, miracles, healing, joy, and rapture. Here we are part of the mind of God, an extension of 'all that is'.

As we evolve, we integrate and experience ourselves as more of a whole. Within us is the wholeness toward which we are all evolving. At some point we can take a leap into this wholeness. Otherwise we will have to step through every single conflict using forgiveness, acceptance, letting go, joining, communicating, integrating, trusting, commitment, giving, receiving, and all of the other transformative methods. Whenever we heal, two or more conflicting goals, selves or parts of our mind come together and give us a more unified and thus a more successful approach. Integration turns negativity, illusion or evil into positive energy with a unified goal. Of course, once healing has occurred it is only a matter of time before the next level of conflict begins to emerge. After every healing, there is a greater confidence, a greater success as a result of the experience of more wholeness of heart and unity of mind. Sometimes this is just what it takes to give us the courage to face the deeper conflict. As we will experience in the exercise of Way 24 we typically have so many goals at any given time for any particular event, it is a wonder that we accomplish anything because there is so much conflict. Each of these goals represents a different self. Each self has it's own belief system and idea of what would really make us happy. As we evolve, these selves begin to join with other selves, making us more whole and less scattered and fractured. We experience less pain and need less defence to hide the pain. We experience more strength, integrity, peace, partnership and mutuality with others, purity, wholeness, love, light and grace. As a result we become healthier, more abundant and successful, and we feel more love and happiness.

Exercise

1. Take one problem or painful event from the past and . . .

- Ask yourself how many different selves were in conflict that led up to this painful event.
- Ask yourself how many new selves or parts of your mind split off as a result of this event.

- Choose that all of these selves or parts be integrated or imagine them all melting into your higher self.
- Who could you forgive that would release this whole issue? Would you do that so as not to hold yourself back?
- After letting go of the grievance would you ask for the miracle which would release this place that you have been stuck?

Repeat this exercise for a present conflict or problem.

2. The many selves within us each have different solutions to any present conflict which would fit their myriad ideas for our happiness. Of course, at best this solution is incomplete because it doesn't take into account the other selves, it merely wants to dominate them and be ascendant. On the other hand, there is the small voice of guidance within us which would provide a perfect solution even to the most impossible situation. We sometimes experience anxiety when we first sit quietly, listening for that guidance with the clarion call of the ego's many voices. As the ego perceives threat, we experience stress and the wee voice of truth certainly threatens the ego, which is based on repression and dissociation of both the lower and higher impulses.

   Sometimes in really big conflicts, people like to get away to a quiet place, which may be more amenable to listen. Yet even in the turmoil we have made, we can hear if we really want to, because that voice will be as loud as we really want it to be. Our ego feels threatened by this guidance because it objects to anything where it might feel coerced. It tries to establish that its will and our will are the same and different from God's will. It uses our authority conflict to save itself even at the cost of our happiness, sometimes even our lives.

Take time to sit quietly. Listen within. What is it you are being called or directed to do? The answer can bring such joy that all these selves are immediately dissolved into a whole.

WAY 14 Healing Competition

One dynamic of any problem is that it is a form of competition and we are attempting to have someone else lose. We have a core belief that someone always has to lose and sacrifice in order for us to win. A problem is actually a strategy to sacrifice. This may be in order to meet our needs or defeat someone now or later. Our problems become means of negotiation whereby we either seek to win directly or to lose, in order to have someone else lose in a bigger way later – when we consider it more important – to balance the scales. Whenever we have lost for someone in this fashion there is an attitude that they owe us. Such thinking is the basis of what the ego as the principle of separation thrives on.

Competition locks us into the vicious circle of superiority–inferiority which is generated by our insecurity in an attempt to make us feel better. But like any ego strategy, it ends up generating more insecurity than there was to begin with. The extent of competition in our lives speaks of how much bonding we lost as a child. This sets up a belief in scarcity, hence the competition, since there is not enough for everyone. But to the same extent competition balances our wins with an equal amount of sacrifice. While competition speaks of dissociated independence rather than bonding and inter-dependence, it correspondingly and to the same extent contains the fusion or muddling of individual boundaries in a sacrifice–resentment relationship, again set up through lost family bonding.

While competition looks at life as a game of scoring and winning, sacrifice – whether acted out or repressed – is like running through a swamp with cement shoes carrying someone else's luggage.

Dynamically, competitiveness is a form of avoidance which obfuscates our purpose and vision. Winning and thus building the ego, at the expense of another, becomes the primary goal. While this may appear to satisfy, it does not necessarily move us forward. It closes down the opportunity for co-operation and partnership. The ego described in the spiritual rather than the psychological sense is that which always attempts to get more than someone else in some area. It wants us to be the best, the most special one, even if it is being the best of the worst, such as in suffering, illness and tragedy.

Dynamically, competition is a delay and a dis-traction, generated by a fear of the next step. We have mistaken winning for success. Success is more than a game. It takes ongoing dedication, openness, learning and willingness to change to become and remain successful. As champions will tell you, the only real competition is with yourself, to exceed your limits in personal and team best. A good opponent gives you a chance to excel. A game of winning pre-supposes a win-lose basis. Sooner or later we pay for a win-lose game by having to lose to keep the game going – if not now, then later.

Instead of competing with others, which is a false economy built on someone losing, we could invest ourselves in co-operation and taking the next step in partnership. If someone loses we end up paying the bill sooner or later. If we take the next step everyone gets to move forward, succeed and have their needs met. Co-operation uses both the resources of the group and the higher inspiration which comes as a result of joining. A competition, which comes from a belief that there is not enough for everyone, has a *win-lose* pattern and does not move us forward to the next, more advanced level, but typically calls for a counter-balancing *lose-win* pattern. Similarly, competition thwarts intimacy and sharing in favour of one-upmanship. Competition is a sign of an unbonded family, a relationship in trouble, and a workplace not functioning at an optimum level. We think of competition as a sign of a healthy individual and society. But it is actually the sign of an independent, dissociated society caught in roles and sacrifice. We don't realise that there is a healthier form of bonded, co-operative individual and society which is based on partnership, interdependence, greater giving and a much greater ability to receive.

Giving up competition, which is generated by fear, allows for higher ethics, greater integrity, sharing, responsiveness and the success principles of co-operation and teamwork. This also allows us to re-establish and recognise the lines of bonding which do exist. Bonding heals relationships bringing truth while generating freedom and ease.

It is through bonding and co-operation that we transcend the family dynamics and patterns which otherwise run our lives below the level of conscious awareness – entrapping us in fusion, lost boundaries and sacrifice, or dissociating us from others in an *untrue independence* and competition. True independence is a place where, building on our own self-reliance, we can connect with others. Untrue independence is a place where we have covered over old pain and dissociated ourselves from needs in an attempt to protect ourselves from getting hurt once again. Untrue independence is where we adamantly do what we want with little or perfunctory regard for others or the situation around us. Because we are blind to our own needs, fears and feelings, we are naturally insensitive to others and inadvertently bring about pain. This false independence is typically competitive, coming from our competitive, unbonded families.

Competition is the key factor in all power struggles and the hidden factor in all deadness in relationships and life. Such deadness is, typically, a sign that we have withdrawn to prevent others from winning over us. In deadness, even the compensation of hard work is, frequently, about proving that we are the best at something and superior to others. Competition is always a delay, because it is looking for success in the wrong place while distracting us from stepping forward.

Exercise

1. Focusing on your present problem and trusting your intuition, ask yourself:

   The person beside myself I want to lose by me having this problem is _____.
   The reason I want them to lose is _____.
   The reason I want to win is to prove _____.

If the person you are competing with is available for communication, begin communicating with them and continue until you reach mutuality, a place where both of you can win equally. This is the only way to generate success now and in the future without worrying about betrayal and ambush on the part of others and sabotage from yourself.

If you want communication to be truly transformative then, in good faith, share your feelings and take responsibility for them. This means acknowledging that if you are the one feeling them, then they are your feelings and your responsibility. Any attempt to blame the other person, either openly or subtly, will keep everyone in the situation stuck in the pain. Even if the other is responsible, they are not more responsible than you. Blame is an attempt to be in the dominating or controlling position while taking no responsibility. This is immature and leads to tantrums.

It is important to also share the deeper feelings such as the fear and competition. As you talk about, or share how these feelings have been a part of your life, there may be memories of key events from your past that surround this feeling. It is acceptable to share these key events, but do not get caught up in telling the details of the story. Keep your focus on the feelings and moving through them because this is how the healing occurs. If healing took place by talking about the details of the story, you would not be in this pain now. As you share these feelings, at the least, one major layer of this pain will be dispersed; at the same time the other person will be inspired to compassion and support for you because of your openness and authenticity. If it is not appropriate to share the memories of the past surrounding your feelings, share only what you can. Now acknowledge your mistake and commit to a new way of being.

If the person is not available for communication because of distance, death, or other reasons, and you are willing to move beyond the competition to get through the problem, imagine yourself building a bridge from your heart and mind to theirs. Choose to forgive them or what you wish on them will be visited on yourself.

2. Imagine yourself in your youth. Commit to equality with brothers and sisters, friends and

peers, teachers and coaches. Commit to equality with those you love or had a crush on. Commit to equality with your parents so you are not the victim of their process. You can voice your feelings of what you want and you can be respected.

Now imagine yourself when you reached adulthood. Once again, commit to equality with brothers and sisters, friends and peers, teachers and coaches. Commit to equality with all of your love interests. Commit to equality with your parents so you do not need to discount them to prove that you are better. Equality will cut through a lot of the sacrifice you may be in with them, especially with regard to them becoming senile or completely dependent on you. Equality allows you to keep enjoying and co-operating with your parents, your children and everyone around you as fellow team members. This is a very simple and easy exercise which can release you from the vicious superiority–inferiority cycle and the burden of sacrifice which can only come about through inequality and thus competition.

WAY 15 Healing the Hidden Agenda

There are hidden parts of our mind that have agendas other than those of which our conscious mind is aware. It is one of these hidden parts which wants our problem. When we are working for success and we achieve something which seems other than successful, we have actually reached a success as defined by a hidden part of our mind. When we aim for something other than what is normally defined as success in a situation, we typically hide this from ourselves. There is an old dictum about the subconscious which states that what we have, is what we want. This can be a powerful way to approach the world because it brings what has been denied, dissociated or repressed to the surface to be resolved. In any problem situation where we blame someone, we disempower ourselves instead of taking responsibility. Our anger or self-attack hides the collusional aspect of our problems.

Let us begin looking for our hidden agendas by realising that we are powerful, purposeful creatures who sometimes make mistaken choices. Everything we do and everything we have done to us fits a certain purpose. When we discover the purpose of our problem and recognise it as a mistaken choice that can never make us happy, we will realise that the payoff is no longer what we want. It is then we can make a healing and life changing decision.

Anything that gives us responsibility while still maintaining our innocence empowers us. Any problem we have is actually a place where we are using the problem to blame someone. It disempowers us and keeps us from examining what is in our own mind. We use it so we don't have to change but we demand change of others. Of course, our changing is the very thing which would help our maturity and success. Yet, all too often when we stop blaming others we fall into the trap of blaming ourselves. Blame is a trap which disempowers no matter where the finger of accusation is pointed. When we venture into areas of the mind which we have kept from awareness, guilt is the common defence the ego throws at us to keep us exploring further. It is important to realise that this guilt is ultimately untrue, and to believe it is to trap and punish ourselves while not learning the lesson or moving on. It is important not to let our guilt stop further explorations or we'll be stuck and not realise that empowerment is a place where everyone is both responsible and innocent.

Exercise

You can intuitively ask yourself the next questions, making guesses where you do not get intuitive responses. To assist your intuition begin each question with:

1. If I were to know . . .

- *What my payoff is in having this problem, is probably . . .*
- *What this problem allows me to do, is probably . . .*
- *What I don't have to do because of having this problem is . . .*
- *What I am afraid would happen if I didn't have this problem is . . .*
- *What I am afraid I'd lose if I didn't have this problem is . . .*
- *If this problem were a complaint, who I would be complaining to is . . .*
- *What would I be complaining about is . . .*
- *Who I am blaming by having this problem is . . .*
- *What guilt I'm trying to pay off by having this problem is . . .*
- *Who I am taking revenge on by having this problem is . . .*
- *What I'm trying to prove by having this problem is . . .*
- *What I'm trying to get by having this problem is . . .*
- *What I am not giving as a result of having this problem is . . .*
- *Who I am rebelling against is . . .*
- *What I'm refusing to obey by having this problem is . . .*
- *Who I am attacking by having this problem is . . .*

- *The need I am trying to have met by having this problem is . . .*
- *The gift, talent or opportunity I'm afraid to embrace which this problem is an attempt to protect me from is . . .*
- *How I get to be right by having this problem is . . .*
- *By having this problem occur, who I am criticising is . . .*
- *What I am criticising them for is . . .*
- *What I must believe that could have brought about such a problem in my life is . . .*
- *The kind of story I'm telling by having this problem in my life is . . .*
- *A problem reflects a chapter of a dark story we are telling in our lives. My purpose in telling this story is . . .*
- *Who I'm trying to defeat by having this problem is . . .*
- *What I'm communicating to all the significant people in my life by having this problem is . . .* (Name the significant people in your life and what you are subconsciously communicating to them).

NAME   COMMUNICATION

When you realise none of these payoffs is making you happy, make another decision.

2. Have a dialogue with the hidden part of your mind. Find its name, age and what its purpose is. Every hidden part of your mind wants to be recognised. In some mistaken way it thinks its misguided purpose could help or save you. Healing begins with bringing to light that which was hidden, denied and mistaken. When you discover what has been hidden, you can help that part choose a better purpose, or a better strategy, and help it join with *what* the conscious parts of your mind want. Simply by realising this hidden agenda is a mistake, our higher mind can begin to change it. You can also integrate that part into the rest of your mind by simply choosing it to do so or imagining it melting into the rest of you to make yourself more whole. Its energy and concern will help you by achieving a unified purpose with the whole of you. This will generate a better strategy rather than many of the misguided ones, such as having you die to get you out of pain, or having you withdraw so as not to be hurt anymore.

WAY 16 Healing Judgement

Every problem is the result of a judgement we are making on the world or someone around us. Not judging a situation allows it to unfold and show its true meaning which is never painful. Judgement, which can never know the whole picture, leads ultimately to pain. *A Course in Miracles* describes our whole world as the representation of our judgement. A problem in the world is a projection of a self-judgement or problem within us. A problem is something we have judged ourselves for, which reflects our guilt. The alternative to forgiving or experiencing feelings so totally that they melt away to nothing, is to stay withdrawn and in denial. We compensate for guilt by acting virtuously, but still project it out through the arrogance of judgement. This keeps us in the hell or purgatory of a problem. Letting go of judgement allows us to have greater awareness and understanding of the meaning of an event and its purpose in our lives. Letting go of judgement allows heaven's meaning to show itself to us.

Judgement shuts down inspiration and locks us into the prison of our own self-judgement. It also imprisons those around us in our perceptions, which come from judgements. When we are judging the mistakes of someone's ego we are looking at him or her through the mistakes of our ego. How can we correct them if we can't correct ourselves? As we judge we imprison ourselves not only by how we see others but by how we return the judgement on ourselves. The quote from the Bible, 'Judge not, lest you be judged', is an accurate psychological statement. Judge not unless you are willing to judge yourself in the same way because you cannot do one without the other. If we judge another we cannot but attack ourselves.

The world with its pain and problems is merely a projection of our self-judgement, self-attack and self-hatred. We do this because of our level of separation from others, from love, joy and even from God. Judgement comes from separation. The amount of this separation and the lack of connection outside ourselves is always a reflection of the disconnection and dissociation inside each of us. This in turn generates the self-judgement, attack and hatred we project and experience in the world. Those we judge in the mirror of the world merely reflect where we are pointing the finger of judgement on ourselves. In every situation where we are tempted to judge we could ask to look at it as heaven would see it. In this way we could be shown a perception where everyone is innocent.

Exercise

Let go of your judgement in this problem situation. It blocks the natural unfolding of the situation, intuition, inspiration and the answer. Your choice to let go allows the problem to show itself in its true light, which is unproblematic. Without judgement there are no problems.

1. Look, feel and listen to your problem. Imagine your problem is a castle. See yourself walking down to a dungeon inside it. When you get to the dungeon, go to the door that seems to be calling you. Open the door and see who's locked inside. Find out their name, how old they are and what they were put in the dungeon for. You can choose to pardon this person or to keep them in your prison, but as you do with them, so will you do with yourself. Ask yourself:

- *If I were to know when I judged myself like this, it was when I was _____ years old.*
- *If I were to know who I was with, it was probably _____.*
- *If I were to know what happened to make me judge myself like this, it was because _____.*
- *Do I still wish to condemn myself for this?*
- *Do I still wish to have this problem?*

Forgiving yourself, and letting go of the judgement on another and self-judgement on yourself frees you. If you decide to forgive yourself, see the person who's been in this dungeon coming up to embrace you. As they are embracing you, see all that they represent

melting into you with all of their energy and
positive qualities, vaccinating you from further
negative judgement in the situation.

2. Ask to see the person or situation through the
eyes of your higher mind. Only with the higher
mind can we see a way forward without losing
our way. If we look and judge through the ego's
eyes we will pay for it because our ego won't
find the way through and we'll lose our way.

WAY 17 Giving and Receiving

Giving makes us successful and the giving of ourselves makes us the most successful. Any problem represents a place where we are not giving ourselves and are somehow trying to take. All problems could be healed by giving. This may be giving in a whole new way, or at a whole new level.

Somehow a problem is the result of not giving, and therefore not receiving, as the two are inextricably bound. There can be no problem in our lives without a corresponding something which we are holding back and not receiving. Usually, with problems, it seems more like someone else is not giving to us. We have complaints because we are not receiving or that what we are being given is wrong. In truth, the problem could be resolved either by opening the door to receive or by giving the part we are called to give. Once you know that any problem can dissolve if you give what's needed, or receive what you yourself and others need, it empowers you to change yourself. This is the power which allows for abundance, love, success, living fully and giving the gift that you are. While sacrifice and compensation mimic giving, you can discern the difference between them because they are not rewarded. Often, because of childhood trauma we withdrew and as a result we stopped giving a certain part of ourselves or being open to receive. This means there are wounded, comatose or dead selves within us and most of these parts are children. Finding those arrested parts of ourselves and reintegrating them can have the whole problem fall away.

As we give, we open the door to receive and also to experience and enjoy what we give and are given. Receiving, in turn, allows us to give at a whole new level. Just as when the student is ready, the teacher appears, so it is that when the receiver is ready, the giver appears. This means that at some level a problem represents a place where we are not yet ready or are fearful of receiving. Somehow we believe that our giving and this new level of success would not only give something to us, but also would take something away. At times we are afraid of losing something, such as a person or indulgence we are holding onto, so the problem actually represents an attempt to not let go. This means we are afraid of the next level of success in our lives, of losing control, of feeling inadequate to handle the gifts or what we are called to do at the next level of success. Sometimes we fear we will be overwhelmed by success or gifts so we would rather not have them.

In truth when we open and receive something new, many times the first thing to come out of us is old pain. This is the pain that previously stopped us because we were too full to let in anything. To let something in requires letting go of some of the old pain. We stop receiving because we become afraid of feeling the old pain and begin to mistakenly associate pain with receiving. But the *letting go of pain* is actually tender and poignant, carrying the sweetness of birth. It takes courage to be so wide open and to receive so much but the more we receive the easier it becomes. As consciousness advances to the higher levels of partnership, such as vision, mastery and enlightenment, it becomes more feminine. The feminine principle is when everything becomes a matter of receiving, so that there is more for giving. After we have balanced the masculine and feminine within us, which allows for committed relationships, we then move into areas where receiving the feminine consciousness gains ascendancy. In this way we advance much quicker and easier. We are now able to move forward even more from receiving guidance, gifts and grace, which is necessary at these higher levels of consciousness, rather than from our own hard work.

Exercise

1. Today, use your conscious mind to examine and give whatever it is that needs to be given in your situation. Imagine the situation and all of the people in it. What is it that each one needs? Give that happily, sincerely and generously. Imagine yourself opening the doors of your mind and heart and giving the exact quality everyone in the situation needs. This sets the positive pattern in your mind, and you naturally follow through with action to embody these gifts.

2. Ask yourself when you closed the door to having whatever the problem seems to be preventing you from having. Therefore as soon as you open this door and receive what you have been resisting, the problem will begin to melt away.

3. Examine what you might be attached to that is keeping your problem in place. What is it you are holding onto? Attachment, which is always a form of trying to get something, can never succeed. Our need blocks our awareness that under the need and grievance, which brought the separation and need about, *there is still the gift of the very thing we've been trying to get*. Only by sharing this gift will the problem be transformed, and when we do the gift becomes a natural part of our lives which we know because we're sharing it. Remember it is not really the form of the gift you want, it is the energy. See yourself sharing that gift and its energy from your mind and heart to whoever needs it around you.

4. Dwell on and discover what it is you're afraid of losing if you were to succeed. The ego typically warns that you will lose something if you succeed and even that you will die. The truth is that when you succeed, it is actually a part of the ego that dies, leaving you with fewer self-concepts, and more openness for receiving and

enjoyment. This is an easy way to move forward. Let go of the fear and be willing to move forward.

WAY 18   Sacrificing Sacrifice

Every problem is the result of a sabotage, which comes about through being burnt out with sacrifice and needing a way to rest or stop. This is a typical ego strategy of a way to give us a break or keep things from being even worse. When we are in great sacrifice we can't stand the thought of another level of success, because to us it just means even more sacrifice. Sacrifice is a form of *lose-win* since, although we appear to be giving, we are withholding ourselves, making it a form of counterfeit giving. Without true giving, there is no real receiving, refreshment or regeneration for us, nor can there be any hope of long-term success. Sacrifice is a form of martyrdom where there is an aspect of the tragic hero. Because this is a role, the hero is tragic in that he is not known to those around him, though sometimes in his trouble he is quick to appeal for the approval or sympathy vote. Unfortunately, because it is a role, an imitation which only mimics true giving, sacrifice cannot fully satisfy, heal or save. It states in *A Course in Miracles* that Jesus committed the last sacrifice so that no one ever needs to sacrifice again. But his followers, misreading the message, as so many followers have done, decided to imitate him. Sacrifice is a psychological trap. Unfortunately when we sacrifice, those we love follow in our footsteps and sacrifice themselves just as we have. Since they love us, they, too, follow us as a way of showing that they love us. Many have attempted to sacrifice out of love for friends, family and partners. Many have sacrificed themselves in a mistaken attempt to save others when sacrificing wasn't necessary. This is a dynamic I've often run into in catastrophic illness. Even when it seemed necessary to sacrifice ourselves, it was just a chapter in the Sacrifice Story we were making out of our lives.

Sacrifice is built on guilt, unworthiness and value-lessness. It denies that we and others can win at the same time and demands that one of us must lose and sacrifice. This is a belief that supports the ego which does anything to keep us from joining and enjoying mutual giving and receiving. Actually, sacrifice is competitive in that it loses now to win later. It fears equality and intimacy, placing itself either above or below the one for whom the sacrifice is made.

Problems are a form of sacrifice. Sacrificing is a role played to protect us from old, unfinished pain. This role is a way of defending against incomplete mourning over loss from the past. Sacrificing is not only an unsuccessful behaviour, it is, even more, an unsuccessful pattern in our lives, separating us from others, and so belying partnership and stopping us from moving forward.

Sacrifice is unnecessary because we can succeed without having to sacrifice. Our beliefs in sacrifice as a successful strategy to keep ourselves from rejection or to make up for guilt, unworthiness or failure merely increase these emotions. Only by facing and healing these feelings can we be free of them and the roles they engender.

Roles and sacrifice were what we did to try and help our original family when they were in pain. This was not only ineffective, it set up some deep-seated, self-defeating patterns and issues. What we've been doing through sacrifice, we could be doing effectively through grace. Through grace we can let go of any roles or mistaken jobs we may have taken on at that time.

Sacrifice depends on ourselves rather than God. The ego uses sacrifice to prove that God wants us to martyr ourselves rather than use grace. Our ego wants us to believe that God wants us to sacrifice ourselves so we'll be frightened of God and His Will. While the bank of God is always open, we persist in the belief in scarcity, dissociation and doing it ourselves. This keeps us so busy we effectively avoid receiving and what we promised to give, accomplish, heal and learn in this life. It is now time to sacrifice the superb counterfeit form of helping and regain love and effective helpfulness. Sacrifice never leads to success. It always lowers our own and therefore others' self-worth. It is a form of giving that always comes from a withdrawn position in which we never succeed in giving ourselves. Sacrifice is a way of hiding from our greatness and our purpose out of fear. In our sacrifice we let others use us as a way to hide how we use them to hold us back because of fear of going forward. Make a choice today for intimacy, balance, self-worth, success and the combined giving/receiving that creates *win-win*. Commit to giving up the defence of sacrifice for yourself and everyone you love.

Exercise

Imagine you could float back in time to where your sacrifice began. Ask yourself:

- *If I were to know who was present with me, it was probably* . . .
- *If I were to know what was occurring, which resulted in me choosing to sacrifice myself, it was probably* . . .

Ask that grace come into the situation and transform it so you do not take on any sacrifice roles or false jobs. The more grace that you allow to come in the more the situation will transform.

With the help of your higher mind let go of your dark beliefs you carried from the past and make a new decision. With the help of your higher mind, ask that everyone in the situation be carried back to their centre, the place of truth and balance. Take your time but ask that yourself and everyone be carried back to as many centres as is necessary to heal everyone. With the help of your higher mind, imagine you are opening the doors to your heart and mind receiving all the grace needed to give everything to heal and transform the situation. You will be freed by your giving and those around you will be freed by their receiving of everything they need.

WAY 19 Peace

Problems reflect stress, a place where our ego or self-esteem feels threatened. Conflicts going on within us, which are causing the problem outside, make more stress. Everything outside us is just a reflection of what is going on inside us. The demands outside us that pressure us are demands we make on ourselves. Perfectionism and what we feel we are supposed to do also add a great deal of stress on us. Dissociation and repression are defences which try to deal with pain and its stress and end up leading to more stress and pain. If we find the inner pain and heal it, the problem and its incumbent stress disappear also. This is why even big problems can be moved through quickly by simply finding and healing the corresponding point of conflict within. If we do not use this approach to heal ourselves within, which emphasises the efficacy of responsibility and empowers us to change the situation for the better, our only alternative is to try to change the situation and everyone else on the outside. We have all tried to change those around us by manipulation, advice and demands, and we all know how rarely it works. Even if we did succeed in changing them through some form of control, they would then become dependent on us, which means we would have to carry them and they would no longer be as attractive. However, if we change ourselves, by finding and healing that part which the problem represents in our minds, the outside will shift easily.

Conflicts are possible only in the absence of peace. Peace is the generative quality from which all good things come, such as love, success, abundance and confidence. It is in peace that our ability to bond and experience love and enjoyment is possible. Not only are conflicts disturbing, they can become the signposts on the road to stasis, suffering and death. When this occurs, sometimes the smallest setbacks or problems can trigger anger, helplessness or depression because they bring with them a feeling that things are never going to change and there seems to be no way out. However, there is always a way if there is enough willingness to change. Peace is the natural outcome when separation has ended. It is peace which can lead us to embrace change with confidence and recognise change as blessed, because it demonstrates that change is for the better, the natural function of education.

Peace extends itself so that the world becomes a benign place and the way through conflict becomes apparent. Conflict just melts away when peace arrives because a conflict both generates and is generated by fear. Peace brings about harmlessness and wholeness.

Many dissociated people shy away from peace, thinking it is either boring or emotionally dead. One afternoon, during the lunch break of a workshop, I dispelled any thoughts of peace being boring when I experienced the deepest peace of my life; it was so thrilling and wonderful I didn't want to move. I spent the next two hours with feelings of peace coursing through me in crests of joy. My inner and outer senses were completely engaged and I was happy beyond words.

Exercise

1. See your problem in front of you and say, *I will not see this as a sign of suffering, destruction or death.* I will not use this as an obstruction to peace, but rather as a means to peace.

2. In meditation, imagine your problem in front of you and, while falling ever deeper into yourself, become more and more peaceful. Relax deeper and deeper into yourself. When your peace reaches deeper than your problem your problem will melt away.

WAY 20   Healing Relationships

Every problem is a reflection of our past and present relationships. Healing the problem moves our relationships forward to a place of greater love. We can actually use our relationships with our partner or the persons closest to us to help heal the issue that's in our way.

The problem is a reflection of something problematic or not yet bonded in our most significant relationship, because everything around us, including our work, our children, and our health, is a reflection of our primary relationship. Of course, what is not bonded in our relationship is actually not bonded yet in any relationship for us. We may not be conscious of experiencing a problem in our primary relationship, but everything between us and enlightenment will sooner or later surface as an issue between our partner and ourselves. Problems around us are merely problems within the relationship which have yet to be resolved and, as yet, may not even have been noticed. Given that there is usually a certain rapport and willingness in our relationship, there is also a certain ease and economy to being able to heal outside problems through it. In a committed relationship, every problem that comes up between our partner and us is just something to be healed in order to achieve an even closer relationship. The answer to any problem is always joining, which means giving ourselves and receiving the other. When a problem arises, if our desire is to build another bridge which would allow another area of ease and bonding between us and our partner, then we will see the problem as an opportunity to get closer and our motivation to resolve it will be all the greater. This especially will occur if we have received many benefits and rewards as the result of our previous joinings.

Exercise

1. If your closest partner, such as your spouse, friend, parent, child or sibling is amenable, share with them your goal of using the resolution of this problem as a means for getting even closer to them. Begin with telling them about the problem, as well as focusing on what is going on in your relationship. As you keep talking and sharing your feelings and experiences, some issue which has been between you will emerge. Ask for the help of your higher mind to find and resolve this issue. Keep communicating with the desire to resolve all misunderstandings and share pain and needs without using emotional blackmail, or anything similar, to force your partner into trying to meet your needs.

   (For a refresher on transformative communication, refer to the exercise in Way 2)

   If your partner doesn't seem agreeable to

this sharing, use pen and paper to write the problem down, and then write whatever comes to mind about your relationship until you find yourself focusing on one main issue. Alternatively, you could speak this exercise into a tape recorder. When you find what the problem is between you and your partner, commit to having it resolved so that both of you can move forward. The problem hides a place of need where there has been a spoken or unspoken demand for them to take care of your need or visa versa, but it can be met through a new bonding in the relationship.

2. Now, imagine the problem is a river which separates you from your partner. Feel your desire to heal it for both of you, and imagine that a bridge is being built from your side of the river to their side. As the bridge reaches them, the way is clear for you to join them, to have them come join you, or for you both to meet in the middle. Every time you think of it say:

There is no gap between my heart and yours.

Not only can this bridging move you and your partner to a whole new level of relationship, it can also transform and remove the problem at hand.

WAY 21 Healing Attack and Revenge

Any problem is a hidden, or not so hidden, form of attack. In any problem there is veiled and indirect judgement against another. A problem is a form of victimisation. It is having ourselves be attacked to attack another with equal amounts of violence. A victim can thus attack another while still appearing innocent and for the most part we repress and keep it hidden from ourselves. Besides attack, a problem is also a way of exacting revenge, not only on the one who seems to harm us, but on at least one other significant person. Sometimes as adults we may be getting revenge on someone in the present and someone from the past, such as parents. Yet all the while we have a conscious belief and feeling of being powerless. *I'm getting back at them by having this problem!* is the essence of our attack/revenge attitude. *I'll be hurt, then they'll be sorry, then they'll feel bad; then they'll appreciate me*. Both as a victim and a victimiser, we attempt to take. Realising that we are attacking and getting revenge allows us to find the simple solution to end this problem by letting go of the attack and revenge through forgiveness.

A problem is a form of hurting ourselves to get back at another through guilt and emotional blackmail. It is part of a power struggle in which we are hurt as our next attack. Giving up this most hidden of dynamics allows us to free ourselves from some of our biggest problems and conspiracies very quickly. The first step in this healing and problem solving process is becoming aware of whom, besides ourselves, we are attacking and why we are attacking them.

When we examine the issue around attack and revenge we may be quite surprised at the answers that emerge. It is typically something we hide, even from ourselves. Now that this has come to light, we can decide whether having this problem is worth this attempt to get revenge. Most people being attacked in this way have no idea that our problem is an attack on them. It is also often the case that the person being attacked in this way has already died. Brought to our awareness, the old mistaken choices to attack can easily be remade, because most of the time they are in conflict with our conscious mind already. On the other hand, even in becoming aware of our hidden pain, we may not want to give it up. At this point, it typically becomes obvious that as painful as the past is, and as much as we've been emotionally arrested, we are holding on to the past and using it as an excuse because we are afraid of facing what comes next on our path.

We can be motivated to let the problem go if we realise that an attack on anyone separates us. It is an attack on everyone, including ourselves and those we love the most. We have much greater opportunities for success and joy than revenge could ever give us. There is a whole world that wants to be helped, one in which there could be enjoyment instead of suffering. Even if we are holding on to the problem as an attack on someone who wounded us, we are energetically and symbolically wounding those around us in a similar fashion. The original pain, like our present problem, is a misunderstanding. If it hurts it shows that our needs were not met, but what wounded us was behaviour driven by pain in another. There is a gift still within which, if we had given it then, would have released them from the pain and saved us from taking on their pain as a victim. Even now under the pain we took on, there is still our original gift. Were we to recognise and embrace this we could return to the original event in our mind's eye and give them this gift now instead of attacking them and others by being wounded by them. Our giving this gift is one of the easiest ways to resolve the situation and restore the bonding where the pain and pattern began.

Exercise

1. Ask yourself:

- *If I were to know who I was getting revenge on from the past by having this problem, it is . . .*
- *If I were to know who I'm attacking in the present by having this problem, it is . . .*
- *If I were to know why I'm attacking them, it's because . . .*

It is time to let go of attack and revenge so we can be happy now and get on with our lives at a new level of success.

2. Imagine going back to the situation where you pulled back or felt wounded by this person. What is it that they would need to feel loved and at peace? This gift still remains inside you waiting until you are ready for it. Imagine yourself at that time just before the pain began going inside yourself where your gifts wait in potential. There you will see a door among other doors, but this one is glowing. Open the door and embrace your gift. Now see yourself back at that time energetically sharing the gift or gifts that those in the situation need.

WAY 22 Truth

Self-deception is a fundamental part of any problem. The problem is a result of something we are hiding from ourselves, even though it may be apparent to everyone else around us. Truth clears self-deception.

Truth, freedom, commitment and ease all have the same dynamics. They are different facets of the same force and energy. What is true transmutes difficulties. Truth is like bringing light to where it was dark, so the darkness falls away. It is the same when we give ourselves in commitment; problems fall away, allowing joining, partnership and opportunities to occur. Difficulties and problems seek to prove something good or bad about ourselves, depending on our particular way of trying to gain attention. Where there's truth there's ease, freedom and a sense of support. Truth resolves the problem and the need that was behind it, showing that the underlying fear in a problem is an illusion. Similarly, it dismisses guilt as untrue, as a ruse of the ego to stop, defeat and separate us, rather than have us learn the lesson, join, move on and succeed. Truth shows how to progress, which had been hidden. It bridges the gap between us and others, allowing everyone to be treated fairly and receive their due. Truth creates freedom by undoing sacrifice and restoring confidence.

Truth can frighten us if we believe it brings about loss. We can believe, as Nietzsche did, that the truth is so overwhelming it cannot be withstood, except by art. Yet it is truth which shows us how to advance and in which direction to shoot ahead. It makes life bearable because only with truth can there be improvement. It invites us out of hell by bringing blessed change into the situation in which we were stuck. Truth brings awareness, clearing the denial which keeps a problem locked in place. It allows everything to move into right relationship so there is clarity and the way through reveals itself. Any problem is a way of hiding the truth. Giving up self deception always allows us to make headway.

Exercise

Today is a day to love the truth, to want the truth and to know that truth will free you. Commit to the truth with regard to your problem. It will set you free. Sit quietly and ask yourself, *What am I pretending not to know?* The truth will give you the answer.

Now that you have asked for the truth, your path and your life will be transformed through your sincere willingness to embrace change. It is important to remember that if your life is disrupted, this disruption is the beginning of a birth process. This is exactly what is necessary for the truth to become evident and free you. Just recommit to the truth and remember that these are the most important times to keep your faith. Do not either adjust to the disruption or settle for the problem. Keep your faith as you move through this process and when you arrive at the truth, or the new level of it, you will be much happier.

Today is a day to ask for the truth to come easily into any problematic situation, to ask for the truth to show you the way to freedom and right relationship. When you embrace the gift of truth, which is always being offered, you can share it to help free others. Choose the truth for yourself and for everyone involved in your problem.

WAY 23 From Control to Confidence

Any problem is the result of a lack of confidence. Where there is confidence, there is no problem just something to handle on the way to a new level of success. Problems are a hidden form of control, the opposite of confidence. Fear and conflict generate our need for control, which comes from and is a compensation for unresolved heartbreaks. With control, we typically have an attitude of wanting everyone to win without being hurt, so we subtly, or not so subtly, direct everyone in how they should act so everything will work out. This tends to invite power struggle because others don't want our ideas, even well intentioned ones, imposed on them. We use our problems as a form of control on ourselves and others, to slow or stop movement forward. We may feel threatened by something negative or positive about another, but in no circumstance do we want something to occur which can overwhelm or hurt us. Or we may feel threatened by something negative or positive about ourselves.

Any defence is a form of control which brings about what it is trying to defend against. Our control and problem bring about more conflicts and power struggle and put us more at risk of being hurt than the protection could ever provide. To be safe it is imperative that we give up the control of our defence and instead use trust, joining and the communication which heals control. To control a partner is to use our perception as the defining one, rather than an integration of both perceptions to raise our partnership to a higher level. This integration can occur through trust, sharing, joining, integration or communication. If we continue, and thus defeat our partners, they become unattractive, dull and dependent on us, causing us both to lose.

The answers to problems arrive at the same time as the onset of the problem. This means the amount of time we take to solve any problem is the time it takes for us to gain confidence in the area concerned. Conflict, which generates control, comes from a split mind. Each part wants different things and is afraid the success of the other part will leave it behind, defeated with unmet needs. We usually project the less identified part of the conflict out on our partner or someone around us, making an interpersonal conflict of what was already a conflict within us.

To have confidence means that we are employing the power of our mind to see a positive outcome, and then continue using it to move through any disruption caused by change. The power of our mind has to go somewhere; it will either go to the solution or to the problem. It can be invested in body appetites or creativity. In the midst of any difficulty, we could consciously turn the power of our mind to seeing and feeling a positive outcome. This means that when any situation is not working out, we have been faithless to it and to the people in it. This stems from faithlessness to ourselves, since all doubt originates in self-doubt. It is crucial that we trust in the unfolding of the situation for a positive outcome. Without trust the fear arises, which can generate very negative stories in our lives. The outcome shows how we've been investing our mind. When we bring confidence to any problem, it will begin to unfold in a way that will ultimately, and sometimes paradoxically, work out for us. Confidence isn't blind, it shows us what we need to know and gives us the faith to act expeditiously.

Exercise

Beginning today, and continuing every day until resolution, put confidence in yourself, in the situation and in everyone else involved. If you consider anyone your enemy, put your faith in them and trust that their actions will ultimately be serving you and the truth. As any outside conflict is a representation of the inner, then an enemy represents a fragment of your mind or personality working against you. Your confidence in them and the situation moves both of you out of control and conflict, toward a common goal. This can have dramatic results, such as an enemy completely changing or departing from the situation entirely.

Today eschew all fear thoughts and use your mind to build up yourself and your life. Invest your mind and heart, your greatest wealth, in the solution rather

than in the problem. Every time you catch yourself
in a fear thought, make a choice not to attack yourself and choose what you do want.

WAY 24 Integration

All conflicts result from a split mind, with each part thinking that a different goal will make us happy. If one side of our mind progressed and succeeded, the other side(s) would feel as if it (they) had lost. The conflict outside us, represented by the problem, actually reflects the conflict within us. A problem reflects a lack of integration and demonstrates we have conflicting goals, which are impossible to achieve simultaneously in the situation. The need for integration is so strong that, even without it, we typically mimic *one-mindedness*, thereby denying and repressing one part of the mind whose goal is different than our conscious mind. It is this denied part which is projected outside us and shows up as the problem.

Integration is a fundamental healing principle present in all forms of healing. It is the joining of these different goals, each represented by different parts of our mind into one higher common goal. When integration occurs with a negative or shadow part of our mind, it melts away the negativity and uses the energy for joining which brings the best of both parts into one form. What is negative becomes a vaccination against further negativity in this regard. For example, a self-destructive part of the mind once integrated provides an antidote for further self-destructiveness. As we become more whole inside, a natural confidence, communication and teamwork springs up around us. There are many thousands of personalities and personality fragments within each of us. All of these make up our ego. Actually, each thought typically represents a personality vying for attention and giving us a goal outside ourselves which, it assures us, will make us happy this time. But only with integration will a greater capacity for receiving and happiness be achieved and will we move forward in an evolutionary manner.

Exercise

When you are in a dilemma such as the one a conflict presents, it is important not to choose any of the separate sides of the issue. Integrating (making whole) will leap you forward into a new level, giving you the energy, quality and best of both sides, allowing you to be satisfied, peaceful and able to receive.

You may want to use a pen and paper for this exercise to record your intuition. Discover as many goals as you can for the problem. Say to yourself, *By having this problem, if I were to know what I want to happen it is*_____. After about six or seven reasons come to mind, you will begin to discover core goals hidden deep within your mind. Given the number of goals present in any conflict situation, you could never be happy or satisfied or even succeed in having any of the goals come about because they head off in so many directions.

In the next step, represent each goal by a shape, human or otherwise. Then assign a feeling or sensation to represent each part, such as hot, cold, fearful, energetic. Then you can also use a sound to represent each goal. Finally see, feel or hear yourself giving all these parts of your mind to your higher mind. Imagine all these are put in a big melting pot and heated until the forms, feelings or sounds melt down to a higher form of one shape, feeling and sound. Sometimes it will come in the form of energy once it has melted down. Now, allow yourself to see the effects of this shape, feeling, sound or energy in the context of your life now.

- What is the experience of this wholeness?
- How will it show itself?
- How will it feel to you and to others?
- What will you say to yourself and to others about how this affects your life and the situation you are currently addressing?
- What will others be saying to you about how this affects your life and the situation you are currently addressing?

WAY 25 Complaining Is An Attack on Self and Others

Complaining is an attack on others and ourselves. Complaining attacks our self-confidence and our sense of safety by pretending to have no responsibility or power to change a situation. Complaints are arrogant in that they put the burden on others to change while excusing ourselves as victims of the situation, rather than accepting our collusional responsibility as a co-maker of this situation; it somehow serves us by giving us an excuse, a way to avoid our purpose or not take the next step. A complaint is a sure sign we are not communicating in a way that invites change, because it looks for someone other than ourselves to blame. This is a poor strategy and a bad attitude which attempts to keep us from shifting. Yet complaining is only partially able to cover over our guilt and feelings in the situation.

Rather than looking for the solution, complaining compounds the problem. It implies others are responsible for our happiness, tries to prove our powerlessness, and demands that others do better to meet our needs. It is narcissistic as it includes a hidden grievance about not being treated specially. Complaining is an attempt to control and save us from the pain of the past which wants to show up in the guise of the present. Complaining dims our awareness of the fact that while we are attempting to control someone to change for our benefit, we are actually afraid to change ourselves. It is a sure sign that we are avoiding our power and ability to make a difference.

Every problem we have is a form of complaint and, if it's a big problem, it reflects a tantrum. Our problem states that someone has not done it right – not done things our way – and as a result we have ended up in a difficult position. Our complaint may be about someone in our present or past, either alive or dead. Even if our complaining got us what we wanted, it would not serve us because it would only increase our immaturity and weakness, our assumption that others need to meet our needs while hiding our responsibility and power. While some of us would rather die than complain out loud, our problems are a way to shout them out for us. As an example, every death that isn't a peaceful stepping out of the body, like stepping out of our car, is either a complaint or a tantrum.

Some of us don't realise that our moods, our long faces which we drag behind us, are a form of sulking and petulance which uses emotional blackmail to try to get the world to change for us. Complaining in its grievance, anger and whining is never discrete but affects all those around us, including all those we love.

Getting what we want through complaining says that we don't believe we deserve what we get, since

complaints use manipulation and force to bring
about a result. This will only increase our anxiety
about our value in the long run. In situations like
this, what brings us back to our power and confidence is communication, trust and changing ourselves. If our outside situation seems impossible to
resolve, then it is important to employ inner methods
of healing and transformation, such as choice, forgiveness, integration, giftedness or grace. If our outside situation seems impossible, there is some
responsibility we are not accepting. Instead we are
willing the situation to remain as it is because we
want the excuse and the indulgence hidden within
it.

Exercise

1. Reflect on your behaviour. Where does it express immaturity such as anger, over-sensitivity,
   moodiness or petulance? Where is it that you
   demand specialness?

   How much complaining about others do you
   do in your mind? You could make a new decision for maturity and effective responsiveness
   now.

2. Choose to let go of your complaints now so
   you can move forward. If you give up the complaint, the problem will fall away.

   Ask yourself:

 • *How is my problem a complaint?*

- *What is it I am complaining about?*
- *Who is it I am complaining to?*

In your answers to these questions, whatever you come up with against someone, ask yourself:

- *Would I hold this against myself?*

If the answer is no, you both are freed. Otherwise, you remain locked in the hell of problems, but at least you can continue complaining.

Examine what the complaint is used for, trusting your intuition.

- *How does this complaint serve me?*
- *What is it this complaint allows me to do?*
- *What is it I don't have to do because of this complaint?*
- *How am I indulging myself?*
- *What responsibility am I afraid to face?*
- *What success am I afraid to embrace?*

Let go of the fear and indulgence for real success and enjoyment. Make a new choice about what you want and how you want to live your life.

3. What are you called to communicate instead of complaining, while being responsible for your feelings and the situation you are in?

Recognise any fight is a form of complaining while having a fear of change.

- *Who is it you need to ask for help?*

Sincerely ask or pray for help. Will that the situation be resolved with your whole heart. If you start communicating with emotional integrity about your feelings and your experience, which is not blaming, you will go through layer after layer of feelings until you soon find yourself talking about childhood experiences. When you finish your sharing, the problem, or a whole layer of it, will be gone.

WAY 26 Judging Judgement

Judgement always involves projection. We judge something in ourselves, believing it is not a part of us rather than recognising a part that is denied and hidden. Having done this we then project it out on others, separating from them and excluding them as being less than us and deserving of punishment.

Judgement shrinks our mind, blocking intuition, inspiration, guidance and grace. We then believe that our judgement is correct and we become stuck with the person or the situation as we have judged them to be. This puts us in sacrifice where we feel our attack is justified. Imagine judgement is like a lovesick gorilla chasing us around the house. We run to find an empty room, shut the door and lock it, only to find a big hairy hand placed on our shoulder as we hold the door. This means whatever we have judged, we're now at its mercy, thrown into sacrifice and suffering as a result. This makes us feel attacked and then angry. *A Course in Miracles* states that all the suffering in the world comes from judgement, while letting go of judgement frees us for clarity and inclusion. Our mind is literally full of judgement. We don't realise that before we judge anyone else, we judge ourselves first. This means any errors we perceive in anyone, we make real in ourselves. Then we try to deny or defend in some way so this behaviour is not evident in us. We are called upon to accept rather than judge because what is accepted is let go of, and we move into a flow where we had been stuck.

Judgement starts power struggles because it comes from guilt. The innocent do not judge, but only discern. In their compassion, they see calls for help where others would have judged and so they reach out. Our judgement is an attempt to separate and make us feel superior to others on whom we have projected our guilt and thus consider bad, different and less than us. The more we judge the worse we feel emotionally, and we become exhausted as a result. We try to correct in order to cover over this bad feeling and so take a defence of righteousness to cover our judgement and guilt. We can't correct ourselves so it's impossible to correct another. We're using our ego to correct their ego, which is like the 'blind leading the blind.' Any place our ego leads we will get lost – if not in contentiousness then by lack of vision. There is no problem that doesn't have judgement as a core dynamic. Our judgement is a form of attack on those around us and our judgement gives rise to problems, which are another form of attack. Both judgements and problems generate fear. Both judgements and problems encourage us to look at the world 'through a glass darkly', because there cannot be clear perception where judgement is involved.

Judgement comes from choice meant to protect our ego and self-interests. It is not something imposed on us. Once we learn this, we have the ability to choose whether we will react or respond to someone and this will determine our attitude towards them. We will then realise we hold the power of freedom within us. We can choose to look at something with condemnation in a punishing way or with compassion in extending ourselves. Reaching out can take many forms such as mercy, support, giving, forgiveness, love or letting go of our judgements, but whichever way we choose, we choose for ourselves as well as others. We could ask our higher mind to heal both of our issues. What we have judged in them is evident by our perception and therefore comes from our self-concepts. (See Way 38). If we give up judgement, we will find mercy, perceive more truly, find equality, partnership and success.

Exercise

1. Take a look at what you're feeling. If you are not feeling anything happy then you have a judgement against someone.

    Who is this person if you were to know, and would you choose to forgive them?

    You know when forgiveness is complete because you will experience peace and the situation you were stuck in will begin to change.

2. Take a look at any significant person from the past that you have had anger or judgement against. Your life, relationships and happiness are held up by this and you will hold those you love hostage to this anger or judgement, either

by taking it out on them or withdrawing from them.

Do you want this to continue?

If not, let go of this judgement and ask for the truth. When the truth is fully here there will be no pain or judgement for anyone. Keep choosing to let go of your judgement and ask for the truth. When you feel peace you will know you are free.

You can ask when you began to judge yourself as you now judge this person you feel injured by. You can ask who was there and what was going on that you began to judge yourself.

You can forgive yourself or ask your higher mind to release both you and them from guilt. All guilt can be released if you want it to be released, but it will be released for both of you or not at all. All guilt can be released in this way unless you are using it as an excuse to stay separate or not to move forward.

WAY 27   Healing Self-Attack

Every problem we have is the result of attacking ourselves. Every self-attack, like every attack, is an
attempt to get something. This may be love, attention, to have some need met, pay off some guilt,
handle the punishment we think God would mete
out to us, prove we are good, worthy, upright, or
even not to have to worry about when attack might
come in since we're controlling it ourselves.

All attack that comes at us in the world is a form
of self-attack. Every loss, hurt, setback, betrayal,
failure and disappointment, is likewise self-attack.
This self-attack, a function of our ego, results from
the self-hatred we have hidden away and denied,
where it brings about our problems. When the problems are severe enough or when the self-attack
reaches a lethal level, the ego suggests either that
we deserve death, or that we might as well give ourselves a rest from the problem by dying. This is all
a mistake, though according to the ego there are
good reasons for dying. These can include:

- abandonment
- unrequited needs
- heartbreak
- revenge
- guilt

- stress
- disappointment
- fighting
- burnout
- exhaustion and deadness
- stuckness
- mortification
- incredible physical or emotional pain
- valuelessness
- meaninglessness
- authority conflict

However, none of these is a good reason for dying, but a good reason for learning the lesson which would free us from the pain and lead to a new birth. When we feel like dying, we are called to heal and learn so a rebirth can occur. Whatever we are attacking ourselves about, as we do sometimes brutally, it is not the truth.

Wherever we have guilt we will attack ourselves. Where we are innocent we cannot suffer. We keep much of the guilt we have in either our subconscious or unconscious minds because we think the guilt is too terrible to deal with, yet still we punish ourselves. There are four major layers of guilt and even the topmost layer is sometimes repressed. This top layer is what we felt we did wrong or didn't do right. The second layer starts in the subconscious and is tied in with failing to save the family. This layer of guilt blocks grace, being and our experience of innocence and sets up doingness, busyness, valuelessness, competition, fusion, sacrifice and other life long patterns of self attack. The third layer of guilt goes into the unconscious as we deal with what is passed down inter-generationally and what our soul brought in as its pattern to heal. The fourth and final layer comes from the mistaken belief in our separation from God. What separates from God is against God. Separation generates conflict and if we believe we are against God, attacking God, then we believe God is against us and we will, besides guilt, also experience fear. This mistaken belief that we are attacking God is the authority conflict at the root of all guilt. It sets up the pattern of soul, ancestral and family guilt, which sets up the patterns of guilt for what we did or didn't do. The ego is built on this fear, guilt and belief in separation, it then projects on God the belief that this attack against him deserves punishment. It proceeds to usurp even this prerogative, which it mistakenly believes is God's attitude toward us, and sets out to punish ourselves to mitigate God's anger.

Logically we have attributed the psychology of an adolescent to the highest force in the universe. God cannot punish, attack, exact vengeance or condemn and remain God. We have projected onto God the face of our own ego and then we punish and attack ourselves accordingly. This attack on ourselves as God's children is an attack on God. If we attack someone's children, we attack them. We mistakenly believe we have separated ourselves from God, but all we have succeeded in doing is to dissociate and repress. Our unity and oneness is still within us, it is just covered over by many layers of fear, guilt,

hard work and valuing what has little or no value.
The experience of ourselves as part of God's Love
is still within us, which is the transcendent experience of the enlightened.

All people have mistaken guilt or self-destructive
areas inside themselves which can be healed.
Frequently, our ego attacks us just after we make
mistakes or just before or after we have our biggest
breakthrough. It saves its most vicious attack for
when we seem to be about to break away from it
and begin to know ourselves as loved and loving.
Often this kind of attack comes just after we have
broken through guilt and pain, let go of identification with the body, or given up our fear of love,
purpose and destiny.

Exercise

1. Every negative thought you have is an attack
   on yourself and increases fear. Make a commitment today to give up your self-attack for the
   sake of the whole world. One of the most
   beautiful passages in *A Course in Miracles* states
   that your willingness to give up your self-attack,
   for one moment, would allow enough grace to
   come through to heal the whole world.

   If you want to help anyone, you are going
   to have to lay down the knife with which you
   have been carving up your own heart. Once
   you lay the knife down, you will also be able
   to help anyone else to do the same thing.
   However, if you keep attacking yourself, the

world will continue suffering and choosing to die. Today, for the sake of everyone you love including your children and all children, choose to lay down the knife. This would be one of the greatest gifts and blessing you could give the whole world.

2. One core way to begin to move past this self-attack identification with the ego is to put the problem into the hands of your higher mind, the creative part of you which has all the answers. In reality there are only two minds – the higher mind with its quiet voice, and the ego with its cacophony. Any thought that is not joyful, healing, or the answer coming in, is generated by the ego. Use this choice to let go and help you move forward:

I put this problem in the hands of my higher mind. I put my future in the hands of my higher mind. I give up my plan and mistaken choices that led me into this place. I forgive myself and will not let my guilt or fear interfere with my answers, and I leave all of this to my higher mind. I open myself for the answer now because I no longer want this problem. I bless myself and everyone in this situation so that we can all move forward together.

The Problem of
Separation

There is no problem which doesn't come from separation. Separation leads to feelings of fear, judgement, guilt and loneliness, feeling lost or orphaned. The orphan is one of the basic family roles based on separation and feeling lost, which we all live out and experience unless we come from a bonded family. We play the orphan role in the family by disappearing so as not to be any trouble, trying to take up as little space as possible, and not to bother anyone with our needs. Sometimes the orphan even gets themselves given away in an attempt to help the family. Our recognition that we played this role and felt this way can surface through our dissociation years later in our adult lives and it can be quite emotional when it does. Separation or lost bonding is one of the key dynamics which gives rise to all negative feelings. Where there is separation there are problems and pain. On the other hand, where there is bonding there is success and love with ease. Most of the time we don't realise that the separation that comes from and leads to judgement is at the heart of our problems, leading to fighting, competition, no connection and feelings of deadness.

The traps of roles and personalities emerge from separation. They are attempts to get approval and value so that we are not excluded. They are a form of counterfeit bonding which leads to sacrifice, conflict and compensation and dissociation. Joining, which is the opposite of separation, and that which joins us to others such as giving, receiving, sharing, forgiveness, acceptance, integration and commitment, all bring about healing. Everything else leads to pain and suffering. If we want to keep improving our lives, it is important to join mind to mind with others. This doesn't mean necessarily agreeing with someone if they are acting crazily, but it does mean bringing the differences together, ending the distance which leads to judgement and the judgement which in turn leads to more separation. Joining ends the separation and as a result, answers come about with a new level of partnership.

It is important to end the differences that now spring up in our lives because they result from lost bonding in the past, which could be re-established with present joining. The withdrawal from life we have made in those circumstances is affecting us now as pain, lack of success, scarcity and sacrifice. Any of these feelings are a sure sign of lost bonding, withdrawal and separation. We have virtually removed ourselves from ourselves, life, parents, siblings, partners, children, friends, our purpose, our meaning, our body, love, success, creativity, work, play, happiness and ease. All of this leads to pain and dragging through life rather than celebrating it. It's time to end the separation and win back our bonding, confidence and sense of connection.

Exercise

Choose from the following list and take some time to heal the separation and withdrawal. Let us take the example of your father, and say you imagine or intuitively guess you are twelve metaphorical steps away from him. These are the steps that add up to all the problems, misunderstandings, grievances and pain that might be between you and having a happy, loving relationship. If you are twelve steps distant from your father and you join with him, you'll step to a new stage in relationship with him and life in general. This allows you to not use him to hold yourself back because of him and it empowers both of you. Of course, it is not unusual for a new, buried level of separation to come up with regards to your father, but with each succeeding level, the joining needed is usually less and you reach new levels of confidence and success. It is normal that old fractures and separations emerge as we keep evolving and healing, but as we continue to join, our lives progressively get better.

In the following categories, ask yourself intuitively *what led you to remove yourself from this person or issue and how many steps you are from a new level of relationship.*

	You Withdrew Reason and Incident	Distance in Steps
Category		
Self		
Life		
Mother		
Father		
Brother		
Sister		
Lover		
Children		
Friend		
Health		
Teacher		
Love		
Success		
Money		
Body		
Sex		
Happiness		
True Love		
Purpose		
Meaning		

Now choose one of the categories, such as the distance from yourself, and ask when you withdrew in that way and by how many steps. Imagine yourself back at the original incident and be that many steps distant from yourself. Now imagine yourself back there and ask yourself what is holding you back from joining yourself again. Be willing to let go of whatever it is and take a step forward. Now ask yourself what is holding you back at the next step, and so on. Be willing to let whatever is holding you back go until you completely rejoin with yourself once more. You may want to repeat this same exercise again at a later time for yourself so that you keep your life moving forward step by step.

Choose another category and repeat the questioning and stepping forward until you feel joined with the next issue or person in the category column. Do this at least once more. Sometimes with a chronic problem you can do this once a day about the same person or issue and you will find things improving level by level and day by day.

This exercise has great effect in changing patterns, feelings, confidence and the world itself into a much more benign place. It can once again begin the evolutionary process in your life.

WAY 29 Healing Projection

Years ago I found an old, but radical concept which proved to be of immense therapeutic help. This was the principle of projection which, followed to its furthest possibility, states that the world itself and the people in it are a reflection of our mind. In counselling as I was looking for 'what worked', I found this concept to have amazing and practical results in helping people change and free themselves when they were trapped. Realising the world is a projection means the most difficult situation or person can eventually be healed, if the aspects of the mind which are reflected outside us are healed. It also means the inner and outer worlds are connected and that the outer is a reflection of the inner. Using this approach has sometimes brought the quick and easy dissolution of major problems. At other times, it has meant a steady healing, layer by layer, and a step by step movement forward. Along with other healing principles and methods, the healing of projection has become one of the most powerful transformational concepts to help change our world. At times this principle has led to spectacular results.

Projection can be especially easy and effective with a significant person around us who has some quality or behaviour which really gives us a problem. What we see in them is something we've projected.

When we find something we don't like about ourselves, we feel guilty about it and try to hide it. We
bury what we feel bad about and then project what
we judged ourselves for onto another. Many times
we disguise the territory and even act in an opposite way. For example, we may have been very jealous
but buried our jealousy to act as if we are independent, dissociated and indifferent. We would then
act in ways that generate jealousy in our partners,
because being insensitive to our own feelings makes
us insensitive to others.

The mind will either project judgement or extend
love. Projecting gives us a dark, fearful, problematic
world. Extension gives us a world of love which is
bright, benign, happy, friendly, peaceful and abundant. Projection literally paints the world with what
we've judged and feared. This may include gifts as
well as problems.

Exercise

What is the problem or quality in the person or situation that bothers you?

Ask yourself what key negative quality the
problem, situation or person reflects and then use
the following healing techniques daily until all negative elements in your problem are gone.

Pull back the projection, which is what you don't
like in them, examining if you have the same quality,
or if you have hidden and denied the quality by acting in an opposite, compensatory way about it. If
you recognise the same quality in yourself, continue

with the method. But if you don't recognise this quality in you then it is evident that you have judged, repressed, denied and compensated for this quality. This means you would almost rather die than have the quality you are judging. Sometimes, if you have a compensatory style, it becomes clearer if you ask yourself the following:

- *If I were to know when I hid this quality, it was at the age of . . .*
- *If I were to know who was involved in this situation back then, it was . . .*
- *If I were to know what was going on that made me judge and bury this quality, it was . . .*

Instead of choosing to bury this quality in that past situation, continue with one of the following methods:

1. Imagine yourself giving the gift which you came to give, which the other needs in the situation to heal the pain within them. Giving and forgiving in this way changes the self-defeating pattern in your mind, which was at the root of the problem.

2. Realise how you have tortured yourself about this quality and, because of it, built a wall of separation between yourself and others. Choose between continuing the torture (*Do I want to keep torturing myself about this quality?*), or leaving both the torture and wall of separation

behind (*Do I want to step beyond the problem to help the person/ situation I've projected on, and who needs me?*). If you choose to step out of the self-attack to help the other, imagine yourself leaving the torture chamber and going beyond the separation to them and embracing them by giving them the support that would free you both in your giving.

WAY 30   The Power of Gifts

One of the dynamics of a problem is that it exists to hide a new gift, talent or opportunity. A problem is a way of avoiding a gift that wants to be born in us, but of which we are somehow frightened. After I had been a therapist for almost two decades I made a startling discovery: A problem or trauma actually reflects a way in which we block ourselves from receiving a gift, talent or opportunity, because we are frightened of losing the control which a problem offers. To receive a gift or move to the next level of success requires us to let go of a certain amount of control, which we use to hold on because we are afraid. When we do not have the confidence for the gift, talent or opportunity of the next step, we use problems to refuse them. If we think back on our lives, the traumas we have suffered reflect rejected gifts. A past that is still painful speaks of gifts which are yet to be received. One of the simplest ways to heal a problem is to discover and embrace the gift that is being offered to us. Be willing to receive it. The bigger the problem, the bigger the gift. If the fear is too great we will even hide from ourselves what the gift is.

Gifts are part of our being. At one level life is all about the development and embracing of gifts. They become a part of who we are in our lives as we realise them. We then bring these gifts into any situation we enter and they help to easily transform the situation and give pleasure both to ourselves and to others. Talents are gifts we exercise for our own and others' enjoyment, while opportunities are an open door to greater success. As we evolve, our lives can become more about our gifts than about our problems, and our whole attitude toward life will shift. Giftedness is a natural aspect of leadership and it moves us and others forward in an easy way. The giving or receiving of gifts demonstrates a flow for all involved. Both the giver and the receiver are enriched by this interaction and this builds abundance. With every step we take forward, a new gift emerges. Gifts are like tissues in a tissue box, if we take one, we are offered another. Each one we accept makes our lives easier and more radiant, blessing us and those around us. As we continuously share a certain gift with a partner, they will naturally be sharing one with us. While this may all take place on an energetic level, it is nonetheless sweet. After enough sharing we now experience our partner's gift as one of ours and vice versa. When this occurs we both go on to receive new and different gifts which can also be shared. This means that we and our partner can develop gifts all through the relationship for each other and the world, making our growth easy and our relationship thrilling. There are literally thousands of gifts and talents that each of us could receive in our lifetime. Each one moves us further along in the realisation of grace, being and understanding our true self and purpose in life.

Every gift is an answer to a certain problem. Each one moves us past a limitation to greater freedom. As we embrace our many gifts, our lives can become a living treasure for ourselves and those around us.

Exercise

Ask your higher mind today to release any fear of emerging gifts that are incumbent in any problem.

1. See and explore the problem you are facing as a device your mind is using to avoid a gift, talent or opportunity. Once you have dwelt on this possibility, use your intuition to discover what gift, talent or opportunity you are being offered which your problem blocks. Once you are aware of what it is, embrace it. See, feel and hear it entering you. It may feel as if it is coming from either outside or inside yourself. Sense it filling you energetically, right down to a cellular level. Now see yourself sharing it with another. How do you and they feel as this happens? What are others saying to you and what are you saying to yourself as this occurs?

2. Another method of clearing the issue is to imagine yourself putting the problem into the hands of God. In doing this, you are gifting the world with the disappearance of one more illusion of suffering. Then see God placing a gift in your hands in return. Let this gift fill you on all levels.

WAY 31 Your Past Is Your Excuse

Understanding the principle that we can be using our past as an excuse saves a lot of time. If we do not take the opportunity to learn this, it is only because we have some agenda to delay our gifts, purpose and destiny.

One way to examine our past in terms of its underlying dynamics is to examine how we are using it in the present. One of the most powerful ways to understand any problem is to examine it in terms of what excuse it provides us, either to do something we otherwise wouldn't have allowed ourselves to do, or not to do something we didn't want to do.

Let us imagine that our past merely gave us an excuse in the present to hide or indulge ourselves in a way we never would have allowed ourselves otherwise. We feel we need our memory of our past, which rarely has anything to do with accuracy, to support a certain line of thinking, rationalisation and justification. Using the past as an excuse is a way of not having to face our fear or feelings of inadequacy, which we use to deal with certain areas in our lives like relationships or integrity. Our past gives us a pardon to renege on our soul's promise to contribute to the earth in a certain way. We think that after what happened to us in the past, anyone would pardon us or find our behaviour excusable, if somehow we didn't show up as we promised we would. Naturally, we tell ourselves we have done all we could, but there were extenuating, defensible circumstances which stopped us. Because of what occurred in our past, we have relieved ourselves of both our responsibility and accountability. And of course any indulgences along the way are exonerated because of what happened to us and because we all have a one-way ticket clutched in our hands so we'd best enjoy the ride. Basically we have given ourselves a 'carte blanche' to do as we please because of our past.

Psychology is meant to bring about the understanding that abolishes fear, restores bonding and lets go of loss for a new beginning. But today all too often we use our past and our psychology as an alibi for our present lack of courage or responsibility. Long ago, we blamed the devil for making us do things for which we didn't want to take responsibility. Now it's our past or subconscious that makes us do it. Yes, our past and our subconscious minds do influence us, but they don't make us do anything unless we want them to or stop us unless we let them. We still have choice in every situation. This doesn't make us guilty, it restores our responsibility and our power.

Anything that lessens our responsibility or increases our guilt weakens us. When we lessen responsibility, we increase indulgence, sacrifice and guilt about the past. This keeps us afraid of the future, thinking what is ahead will turn out like the past. If we use the past as an excuse, we will never accept responsibility or maturity, and without these there is not much hope of happiness; we will be bandied about on the waves of fate or at least we'll portray ourselves in this way. We will never know the power of our will, have the courage to obviate the past with vision or experience the mastery of being in the here and now, and we will never know the fulfilment of contributing our purpose or the happiness of living our destiny.

Exercise

1. List three painful happenings from the past.

- What is it they allow you to do or what is it you don't have to do as a result?
- What present excuse do you have because of this event?
- Examine three indulgence areas. Ask yourself what has occurred that gives you the excuse to have this problem or indulgence.

Past Event	Excuse	Indulgence
1.	1.	1.
2.	2.	2.
3.	3.	3.

If you no longer wish to use the past as an excuse, you can let go of the excuses and the past and ask your higher mind to replace them with truth. See yourself putting your past and excuses in the hands of God; see and feel what you are given in return.

2. Now is the time to make a new commitment to take responsibility and use the power of choice.

• Here is an exercise that can help. Let's say you are not feeling happy. Take responsibility for how you are feeling and simply choose to feel happy. Note any changes positively or negatively. Sometimes in a chronic bad feeling, feelings may get worse before they get better. You may want to write down how you are feeling and the result of your choice.
• If you're not feeling happy yet, repeat the process.
• Note once again how you are feeling and write it down, if you choose.
• Once again take responsibility and choose happiness. Experience what you are feeling and write down the result of the choice.

Do this as many times as is necessary until you feel happy, creative, loved or whatever it is you want. When you are finished, read through your process. People who have to go through many layers of feelings not only become much more aware of their transformational process, they also report significant changes when they are through.

WAY 32 What We See Is Our Past

If we are not happy, we are replaying the past in the present. This process has been recognised by psychiatry with the term 'transference.' Basically we keep replaying the past until we get it right. We face similar emotional challenges until they are met. If we don't learn the lessons, the past will come up again and again masquerading in different disguises as a present situation. We must deal with our patterns and other unfinished business until they are resolved. If we have not learned the lesson but compounded the pain by an emotional reaction, then it will be a trial the next time we face it. If we realise the implications of transference, we can begin to see that one of the functions of life is for us to heal. If we do not heal, problems will repeat from family to relationship situations and from relationship to victim situations. Without a healing attitude we will try to avoid our problems rather than transform them. With a healing attitude we take the power to have a good life back into our own hands. As we forgive, let go of the past and heal its mistaken separation with new bonding, we move forward in our lives with greater confidence.

Too many times we push ourselves, just going

through life without even bothering about whether we feel good. We only stop and take notice when we start feeling bad and something begins to be problematic for us. If we realise bad experiences and negative emotions don't just occur but emerge as we are ready to heal them, then equipped with such awareness we can become more motivated to heal them. Of course, with any lesson or negative experience our ego wants to build itself up and attempts to compound the pain and further raise its walls of separation. If we take an attitude of healing and we know that anything which comes up is our past wanting to be healed, using people in our current situation to replay old roles with unfinished business, we can then be motivated time and again to heal our present situation.

For success in life and love it's important to take a healing attitude toward anything which isn't happy and to commit to learning the lesson of the past in the present once and for all.

Exercise

The following exercise is very good at getting to the root of what's going on. When you finish with the exercise, if you are not completely at peace, then there is another older and deeper layer to heal. Proceed until you're fully at peace. Choose a problem or painful situation and see what pops into your mind when you ask the following questions:

- *If I were to know when this began, it was probably at the age of . . .*
- *If I were to know who was involved in the problem, it was probably me and . . .*
- *If I were to know what occurred for this problem to begin, it was probably something like . . .*

In this original scene where the problem began, imagine the light inside you connecting with everyone in the scene. Now see how the scene unfolds. If it is not yet a happy scene, imagine yourself reconnecting the light within you to the light within everyone. Repeat this until the scene finally becomes healed and then happy.

If the incident seems to refuse to get better, it's because there is an earlier incident that is in the way. Ask yourself the above questions to get to the real root of that scene which doesn't seem to resolve. It is unlikely you have to do this more than twice, though it has sometimes happened. Many a person has gone back to three years old (the most common age for trauma), only to have to go back to birth, or even to a time in the womb or at conception to fully resolve the pattern. At times people have dealt with ancestral issues passed down through the family or even soul issues brought into this life. While this may sound utterly fantastic to you, it has become an everyday experience for me. When these deeper areas heal, whether or not the stories which emerge are imagination or actual fact, people are released from painful patterns and they become more successful in their lives and relationships. You can use the healing exercise effectively wherever there is a separation, which means when anything less than happiness and success is occurring.

WAY 33 What We See Is How We Used to Be

We see the world through our perception, which when negative comes from our past, unfinished and unintegrated experiences. We bring feelings and perceptions that belong in the past into our present situation for healing. All we ever see is the past, *unless* we're experiencing love, appreciation and happiness. This can be explained in a number of ways. The first is the transference level of interpersonal relationships, where we bring everything unfinished from past relationships to the surface to be dealt with and resolved. A second deeper level that can be addressed is the intra-psychic level, which is going on simultaneously. This is the level where the soul reflects or mirrors our mind back to us in the world. This is a level where all attack in our world is a form of self-attack, a reflection of the conflict and self-attack in our own mind. To heal either of these levels of the mind, whether we're carrying what's unfinished from the past or the world is being mirrored back to us, will allow us to heal the situation and all the levels of the mind completely.

Our perception comes from the unfinished business or from the level of projection where the world mirrors our mind, representing what we believe about ourselves. At some level all thoughts, unless creative, are generated from personalities which are the self-concepts or beliefs about ourselves. Each thought or concept we have reflects a self-concept. At some level all we experience in the world is ourselves, our thoughts and perception coming from self-concepts. We see and experience the world in terms of self-concepts about how we used to be. This means that when we forgive someone in the world, we literally and metaphorically forgive ourselves.

Let's review this. At the interpersonal level, the relationships we experience are made up of past relationships where we have not yet learned a certain lesson. And any situation in the world represents a number of past relationships mixed together. Our present relationships represent the transference of past relationships into the present. Now these same relationships and situations at a deeper level represent how we acted in the past and self-concepts we have carried over as a result. These self-concepts at both subconscious and unconscious levels of the mind are how we acted before or how we thought we behaved. So if the world is problematic, what is before us at one level is the pattern of our past relationships before us once again, and at a deeper level the problem reflects how we used to be, our self-concepts that we judged, rejected, and repressed. The world before us is thus a mirror and as we pull back and heal our projections through joining, forgiveness and integration, what is in front of us in this mirror seems to change in front of our eyes, becoming more benign and whole.

This mirror principle once understood becomes of great benefit in helping people change their painful experiences, including self-attack, judgement and conflict with others. It helps us take a level of accountability about what happens to us as we begin to realise what we are doing to ourselves. It throws new light on such old statements as 'What goes around comes around' and, 'You reap what you sow'. Over the years the mirror principle has greatly helped many people to forgive and re-integrate their old hidden selves into a new whole, bringing about less fear and conflict for them. The problem with these old selves and self-concepts is that they are not integrated or assimilated and so are not unified, and this is reflected by others around us going off in different directions. Because we judge and dissociate or repress selves, they come into conflict with the self with which we identify or become like anchors which we drag behind us. As these self-concepts have different ideas about what to do and where to go to be happy, they set up conflict within us and thus with others outside us. People that we are in conflict with represent inner selves with behaviours, emotions and logic systems which we judge, repudiate and fear. Those conflicts occur with certain gifts, talents or problem selves which we thought we couldn't handle. This led us to suppress or repress the gifts or shadow 'selves'. To put it simply, what we see in the world is us and how we used to be, now judged and separated both within us and outside us.

Recently I worked with someone who had a

member of his family who was angry and had a negative attitude. Using the intuitive method I asked the person I was working with where this negative energy began for them, as reflected by the person in their family, and we ended up with two incidents at three years old and birth. While you wouldn't guess that we even have a mind developed enough to have experiences which pattern us psychologically at birth, in the womb or at conception, what I can tell you is that for nearly three decades I have seen people report these incidents, and as they cleared them, a significant difference occurred in their relationships and their lives. This person cleared these old incidents through centring and gift giving, and later reported that the family member seemed to have changed and become more peaceful.

When we judge something about ourselves we either attack ourselves or try to suppress, repress, or pretend it's not there. Then we project it out on the world in an attempt to put distance between us and this quality about ourselves. If we see it in the world around us, we typically judge or attack it, as we have already done with ourselves.

Reflect for a moment on the principle that the world around us is made up of rejected parts of us separated off by pain or judgement. This is why at times when we get close to others, layers of painful emotions can emerge either triggered by something obvious or seemingly for no good reason. It is the pain or bad feeling that keeps the separation going on the outside and the corresponding split in our minds on the inside. Because we are afraid and

unmotivated to face negative emotion, we separate
from those people on whom we have projected out
a part of ourselves. If we imagine we are similar to
what is around us in the world, we can feel an
emotional reaction, perhaps denial, guilt and sometimes anger. But once there is forgiveness or understanding of those outside us, there is recognition of
how we are all joined.

It would be helpful to practise the mirror principle consciously for a while by looking at the world
as if it was what we were asked to forgive. 'Everything
outside of me is how I used to be. The world shows
me selves which I rejected'. If we can 'own' a certain person's behaviour as our own, if we can identify with a certain person's behaviour or emotion as
ours, then if we choose to not hold it against ourselves we are free and so is the other. We will have
successfully accepted this aspect and let it go as no
big deal. This has the same power as forgiveness and
integration to free ourselves and others. In this way
both we and the person we saw the negativity in will
move forward. We will no longer have this quality
within us going in a conflicting direction as a hidden
agenda and we will easily be able to support those
who have fallen into similar traps with their incumbent self-torture. If we react, deny, threaten or in
any way get defensive about this quality within us,
then we have a compensation over the old judgement of this self. This means we are in sacrifice,
acting out a positive role, but receiving no reward.
To transform something in the world that we are
having a problem with, which is actually part of us,

can have a major transforming effect on how we feel about ourselves, our confidence, self-love and happiness by letting go of sacrifice and receiving at a whole new level, not to mention its ameliorative effect on the world. But it seems clear that we will either get through a problem together with another person or we will both keep the problem and the conflict. Whatever we do will be done for both. We can take the opportunity now to heal this person who represents us.

Exercise

Take a person or situation around you with whom you may be having problems. List the negative qualities you experience about it or them.

1.   4.
2.   5.
3.   6.

See the person or situation you have been judging. Now reflect on whether you act like that or you'd rather die than act like this, a sure sign you've compensated. Notice that with both styles you still attack and torture yourself as a result of this self-concept. Now choose if you are going to keep torturing yourself for this or if you are going to pull yourself or selves out of the torture chamber and go help the person you have been judging and projecting on. If you choose to support them, it will have the effect of re-integrating the negative quality so you will see them differently and feel better yourself. Do this same exercise with each negative quality you see in the person or situation.

See the problem person or situation in a full-length mirror in front of you. As you are watching them or this quality, see the mirror begin to change back to when you used to be like this. If you are willing, welcome yourself or selves out of the mirror and into your embrace. As you do this, feel them melting back into you, reintegrating the lost part. When this is complete see how you feel about that problem person or situation now. If it feels incomplete repeat the mirror exercise until you feel good and your perception of them and yourself has changed.

WAY 34 The World You See Is What You Choose to See

This chapter explores one of the most hidden aspects of our mind and in some ways is a review of the essence of the book. Our world and our lives are unfolding according to our choice. Just as all dreams represent wish fulfilment so our everyday lives – our waking dream – represent wish fulfilment. Or to put it another way, what we see and what happens to us and how we experience it equals our choice. Given the dark circumstances and situations which appear in the world, it could only mean that we had corresponding dark thoughts in our own minds. Where these dark, painful places abide in us, like beliefs, there is an automatic choice which brings about the world we experience, much like a program running a computer. It is these broken places within us which we have come to heal so as to heal the world. When trauma happened to us in our lives because of these dark places in our minds, and nothing was healed, then these experiences which fade or are repressed as time goes on, continue to program us and our world in a negative way.

We are now approaching a time in our world and social development where we are once more ready to open up and deal with the unconscious mind. All civilisation at one level is an attempt to keep the unconscious at bay. In the western world we have been stuck at a step in development I term the 'Dead Zone'. This is a place where we are living our lives while working hard to keep the status quo but feeling as if we're caught in a rut. There are many things going on here but the Dead Zone is partly a defence against the unconscious, which we all started cementing over between seven and fourteen years of age because of our terror of this more powerful, primitive and, at times, shamanic mind. Now is a time where partnership, leadership, vision, and mastery are needed. It is a time where guides for the unconscious are needed, which is a simpler mind than the subconscious, filled as it is with family, relationship, and victim dynamics. To understand and traverse the unconscious mind is to learn first hand of the demons, dragons, and treasure there. The events of terrorism in America on September 11 2001 are an example of the unconscious erupting into everyday life. Because we are close to the jumping off point to interdependence, which is what tames and focuses the unconscious, the defence of the Dead Zone is wearing thin. The shadow figure of the 'terrorist', one of many shadow self-concepts, broke through and in a very vivid and real way terrorised and brought tragedy. This is a time when it becomes crucial to win back parts of our mind to empower us. Choice is the most powerful human tool available to us.

It is well accepted that we ourselves are programmed not only by the painful past, but also by how we then experience and interpret what happens to us in light of that past. But the principle of choice in this chapter has even more far reaching implications. The foremost philosopher of the last century, Martin Heidegger, described man as a being-in-the-world, inextricably bound with our world. The implications of this concept are that what we choose not only affects and effects us but the world also.

The subconscious and unconscious minds are made up of all that threatens the ego. This means there is a lot that is unintegrated and hidden from our conscious mind, which leads to conflict. These experiences which are either too light and transcendent for the ego to handle, or too dark and destructive, were all labelled as threatening to the ego which likes to maintain our status quo. Whether or not these repressed elements are recognised, they still continue to generate the experiences and stories that we live in our lives. Beliefs and images in our minds are like static, continuous choices which are always going on and they have an effect not only on us but also on what happens to us.

The reason these old images and beliefs aren't always generating something very positive or very negative at any given time is that the ego defends against such experiences, so as not to be overwhelmed. To do this it expends a lot of energy for defences, which would otherwise go to the experience of joy, which is also threatening because of its ego-melting ability. When necessary, the ego uses the dark, shadow area of the unconscious to attack us and defend against light transcendent areas because in this part of the mind, which is light, the ego is unnecessary and would meet total transformation or even dissolution. This basically keeps a balancing act while delaying us as much as possible.

The ego uses guilt to keep us from wanting to explore, heal and embrace the power of our mind, which would eventually make it obsolete as our higher mind took over. The ego translates accountability and choice into guilt and blame. If we can't blame someone else, the ego simply blames us to achieve the same effect of maintaining its control. To attempt to keep us out of our own minds, the ego translates any responsibility as guilt, which it then tries to pawn off by projecting guilt and the need for punishment on someone else. In the United States, this has led to a litigious attitude where we have gone overboard in assigning other people guilt for what happens to us. We make others guilty, not only for what happens to us, but also for what we *feel*. A healthier attitude, which would empower us, is that of total co-responsibility. In response to the ego's use of guilt to keep us out of the subconscious, our higher mind has a learning curriculum all set up for us with which to grow and progress easily and gracefully.

As I have worked deeper and deeper in the mind, at first exploring the hidden factors regarding relationships and then delving into the subconscious and unconscious mind regarding all elements of the victim experiences, I have found that relationships are all no-fault in that we are all one hundred percent totally responsible. For instance I have found that where someone in a relationship seems to use us or harm us, the whole situation is collusional and that we are using others to attack us and hold us back because of our fear of life, intimacy, and the next step. As we take responsibility for our lives and relationships, we begin to understand our hidden agendas. Our understanding and responsibility empower us and move us forward in our lives. When all the circumstances finally come to light and become fully understood, then all the guilt and grievances are naturally released. At this point a certain gratitude emerges that the world and our lives can be understood and that we have the power to change circumstances we do not like. We tend to think that life is just happening randomly, accidentally and chaotically but there are principles which, when understood, can be used to move ourselves forward. This learning is, of course, anathema to the ego which builds itself through victims, perpetrators, judgement, guilt, blame and pain, and wants to delay or stop us from moving forward.

What could possibly make us want to choose such dire, traumatic experiences and victimisations? For the last twenty-seven years, since I learned ways to access the subconscious, I've been exploring through my own mind and with victims what brings about our troubles. Presented here are some of the major mind dynamics, which serve as dynamics for victimisations. This list includes some of the more common but hidden purposes to show up over the last two-and-a-half decades. Typically, as stated earlier in 'Way 10, the Power of Choice', we choose and instantly repress these 'payoffs'. One or many can be extent

in any problem situation. This is not a complete list,
but if you can collapse or heal any one of these
dynamics totally, the problem usually collapses. The
following represents about a third of the dynamics I
have found as core issues in problems.

1. To get attention
2. To attempt to have a need filled
3. To allow us to do something we wanted to
   do but wouldn't otherwise allow ourselves
   to do
4. To have things our way
5. To not have to do something we didn't want
   to do
6. Unworthiness and valuelessness
7. Lack of confidence
8. To protect ourselves from fear
9. To protect ourselves from losing something
10. To not have to face the next step
11. A conspiracy to trap ourselves for as long as
    possible
12. To protect our fear of intimacy because we
    feel inadequate
13. Comparison and competition, which comes
    from lack of bonding
14. To try to take or get something
15. To be loved
16. To learn a lesson
17. To prove something
18. To take a shamanic test in the hope of
    leaping to a new level of awareness and
    power

19. To have an excuse
20. To defeat someone
21. To get revenge
22. To avoid our purpose and destiny
23. To attempt to payoff guilt
24. To sacrifice ourselves in an attempt to save the family or someone close to us
25. To sacrifice ourselves to win later
26. To sacrifice ourselves to avoid the next step or our purpose
27. To sacrifice ourselves to avoid our destiny and attack God
28. To not show up
29. To stay small and hide
30. To have our second greatest fear occur so as to avoid our greatest fear
31. To control someone
32. As a reflection of our primary relationship
33. To hold on
34. To try to save our family
35. To rebel
36. To be independent
37. To avoid a gift, talent or opportunity
38. As a reflection of how we treat ourselves
39. To attempt to give a message to someone through what is happening to us
40. To protect ourselves from fear of our greatness
41. To protect ourselves from fear of our self, our higher self, our life or God
42. To attempt to protect ourselves from fear of great pain

43. To attempt to protect us from the unconscious mind
44. Sabotaging success because of too much sacrifice
45. To hide an even deeper conflict
46. To block the truth out of fear
47. To strengthen the ego
48. To attack someone
49. To attack ourselves
50. To protect ourselves from our fear of freedom
51. A family role
52. To be right about something
53. A soul injury
54. To attempt to heal something
55. Repression emerging
56. To hide our fear of death which shows our fear of life
57. The Oedipus conspiracy
58. To hide and keep an indulgence
59. A shadow figure
60. To show how good or bad we are
61. Projection
62. The agenda of a hidden self with a mistaken strategy
63. An idle wish or thought
64. To be special (counterfeit love)
65. Our belief system
66. To be caught in some trap or conspiracy so we don't have to face the fear of our next step
67. A split mind
68. Self deception

69. To complain about something
70. Judgement
71. To demonstrate a grievance about something
72. To try to prove something
73. An unconscious life script or story
74. Bad attitude
75. Fear of freedom
76. Fantasy
77. Expectations
78. Dissociation
79. Separation
80. Authority conflict
81. Shame
82. Self consciousness
83. Meaninglessness
84. Depression
85. Fear of loss
86. Narcissistic need for attention
87. Grievances
88. Misunderstanding
89. Lack of commitment
90. Loss through lack of valuing
91. Withdrawal
92. Anger
93. Fear of sex
94. Fear of success
95. To control ourselves
96. Perfectionism
97. Compensation
98. Unwillingness
99. To attack God, to try to prove we are more powerful and should have God's job

100. Fear of our purpose and our destiny

What we see or experience serves us in some way, even if it is negative. It is following a certain script which we somehow think will make us happy. As evidenced by our lives, we have all at times made major mistakes with regard to what will make us happy. We have used our own ego strategies and got lost. We've wanted to do it our way – to not have to change. We've been afraid to listen within for guidance and afraid we'd have to give up some favourite indulgence or do something that we felt too inadequate to accomplish. At some deeper level every negative experience we suffer is a call for help and a call for love.

The following are some of the main healing principles, which will be addressed more specifically in the exercise:

Healing Principles

- Since everything outside is a reflection of what is inside us, if we forgive ourselves, what is occurring interpersonally transforms to a more successful level.
- If we give or support rather than judge, the situation will change for the better.
- When something negative occurs in our world, we can invoke the truth, which will bring freedom and light.
- We can undo the negativity through choice and the power of grace.

- We can be willing to take another step forward.
- We can let go of attachment, trauma, fantasy, indulgence, negative emotion, judgement, grievances and having our way.
- We can receive grace and channel it to that person who is in need of our help.
- Whenever something negative happens in our world, it is the result of a grievance or judgement and our forgiveness can change that.
- We can ask for heaven's grace and help to transform the fear at the root of any problem.

If we learn these ways of transforming, we will learn that our world is not cast in cement, but that it is as fluid and mercurial as our minds.

Exercise

1. Pick a number between one and one hundred to find the main dynamic holding you back in your life right now.

2. Pick a number between one and one hundred to explore the main dynamic for a problem you are experiencing in your life.

3. Pick a number between one and one hundred to explore the main dynamic for a past trauma in your life.

If you get too familiar with which numbers are assigned to which dynamics, number some cards or put the dynamics on a card and pick from the deck. This takes the conscious mind out of it and allows synchronicity to work.

Now, examine your life, taking full responsibility for it. This means no blame or guilt for anyone, not even you. See everyone as doing the best they could under the circumstances, but recognise that we could all do better.

When something negative happens to you or someone in your world,

1. Ask your higher mind for help to heal and transform the situation.
2. Be willing to be wrong about your perception and experience. Let it go. Ask for and see what higher perception comes to take its place.
3. Make another choice about what you want.
4. If there's something negative then something is not yet understood. Commit to the understanding, which will free everyone.
5. Join so any separation, which is at the heart of any problem, ends.
6. Communicate so bridge-building, understanding and forgiveness comes about.
7. Let go of the judgement that caused you to see and experience something negative.
8. Forgive the one you have a grievance with which gave rise to this problem.
9. Realise if an experience is negative, it's not the truth. Ask for the truth. Choose the truth. Commit to the truth. Love the truth.

10. Let go of any attachment or indulgence that any problem hides.
11. Be willing to take the next step.
12. Put your future in God's hands.
13. Forgive yourself and God.
14. Let go of self-attack and attack on others.
15. Let go of sacrifice, it won't succeed to save anyone or accomplish anything but hiding.
16. Give up self-punishment and the guilt that drives it. It won't pay off the guilt.
17. Let the guilt go to free those you love.
18. Receive gifts, love, grace and miracles from heaven for yourself and those who need help.
19. Trust the process. Your trust will paradoxically unfold the situation positively.
20. Let go of your ego's plan for God's. God has a plan where no one has to sacrifice, not even you.
21. There is something you could give, possibly a soul level gift that is waiting to be realised, embraced and given to change the situation.
22. Hear the call for help by someone around you, which your problem is trying to hide.
23. Integrate all the selves as reflected in your world.
24. Go back to the situation where the root of this problem began. Now end the separation that began the problem.
25. Manifest a positive outcome using the power of your mind through visualising, feeling and sensing.
26. Pray for what you want.

27. Desire what you want with all your heart while giving up any need or attachment.

28. Put the problem between you and someone close to you. Join heart to heart, mind to mind, to dissolve the problem.

29. Commit or give yourself fully as a problem reflects someplace you are not giving.

30. Live your Purpose.

31. Embrace your destiny.

32. Be willing to change and move forward.

33. Realise that whatever negativity is present in your world is the result of some hidden or not so hidden negative attitude. Become aware of what this dark perception in your world reflects about your negative attitude. When you discover it, make the choice to turn around and go in a positive direction. Choose life.

34. Realise that every dark experience reflects what is missing in your closest relationship, in all of your relationships. Realise this is an opportunity for a new level of bonding. Choose to join and love them in this area.

35. Every dark perception reflects a place of unworthiness and valuelessness inside. Put this unworthiness in God's hands and see yourself as a child of God as He does.

36. Every dark perception reflects a self-concept within. Integrate this with your higher self for a new level of wholeness.

37. Bless yourself, the person or the situation that reflects the problem outside you. Eschew any

cursing of yourself or cursing of anyone that may have led to this.

38. The negativity you see reflects some kind of separation. Ask yourself who you can join with, mind to mind, to alleviate this.

39. This negativity you see reflects a promise to help or a gift you promised to give, which you have not yet given. Re-commit to giving that gift or completing that promise, even if it seems way beyond you. Heaven will help.

40. Gratitude and appreciation always set a positive flow and unfolding. This will clear at least a layer of the problem and you can repeat it.

41. Ask for grace and miracles for yourself or the situation. Open yourself to receive these gifts.

42. Let go of any indulgences.

43. Let go of any attachment.

44. Let go of any fantasies.

45. Let go of any expectations.

46. Let go of the past except for its happiness.

47. Accept. As you accept, let go of what was resisted and a flow begins.

48. If there's a dilemma, commit to the next step, commit to the truth.

49. Let go of trying to decide. Ask for guidance and a very clear sign. It will be as clear as you want it to be.

50. Recognise any problem as the result of a split mind. Ask that all the problem elements and problem people who reflect parts of your mind be integrated so a new level can come about.

Now pick one, two or three numbers between 1 and 50, and use this list to find an effective way to change what you choose to see.

WAY 35 Taking Up Too Much Space

The feeling that someone is taking up too much emotional, physical or psychological space in the family can be subtle or so overbearing it is hard to breathe. If the latter occurred, we probably felt we didn't have enough room to grow and develop our talents. We felt overshadowed, as if we were a seedling that had to grow up next to a redwood. If we have experienced this we will be in a conflict about letting ourselves shine and even though we may be an adult and living far away from our family, our ego will convince us that if we shine we will block another's light and keep them from shining. It is then easy to hold ourselves back, falling for the trap of fear of envy, where someone might attack us because of our success. We may not have been fully conscious that we felt someone took up too much space while we were growing up, but it can still be affecting us. It can set up situations where we experience a power vacuum and feel we have to step up because other people feel too unworthy to take their true place and shine. Or we feel that we have to take over and do it all, yet later we feel guilty for taking up too much space or being over important. This conflict may lead us to feel that we are not giving enough space to our lover, spouse or children. It brings us into a conflict between shining our light and simply disappearing.

When we feel someone takes over or invades our space we feel put upon and resentful. The fear of someone taking up too much space can be one of the major reasons we put distance between ourselves and our original family and it can be a factor in keeping us distant from a lover, spouse, parents or family because of the subconscious fear that we or they will take up too much space. The other factor which can influence us to keep space between us and those we love is the fear of being in too much sacrifice to someone's spoken or unspoken needs or demands, while underneath there may be the fear that we would put them in too much sacrifice by our needs or how much space we take up. This can occur because of someone's personality, their fear, illness, or even the importance of what they're doing. Sometimes someone barely takes up any space at all, but then, goes completely to the other extreme through a problem. All of this fear about space and needs comes from lost family bonding and the fear of our purpose. If there is bonding, balance and equality in our family or if we embrace our purpose and destiny we restore most of our bonding and confidence.

These thoughts and feelings about taking up too much space, though hidden, can keep us away from our natural authority and confidence to lead and teach, and even from our power to change ourselves and our world. We can vacillate back and forth between stepping up to fill the energy vacuum which we feel and the guilt we have for being at the centre of attention. Also, if our parents were constantly fighting, we commonly experience them taking up so much emotional or psychological space that we in turn feel prevented from taking our place in the world.

Bonding provides balance and equality in our minds, our lives and our relationships. With it there is a natural confidence, which allows us to be responsive for whatever is called for or needed in life. We can step up to lead the way if necessary and we're also content to play our part on a team. Without the bonding or the willingness to embrace our purpose, we will always compensate, overreact, second-guess, doubt or trip over ourselves to make up for what seems missing in a situation. If we are caught in this conflict we can exacerbate our partner's competitiveness and it may lead them to attack us after the honeymoon stage in the relationship, because it brings up their envy and insecurity. We may feel attacked or blindsided by them and not realise why they are acting like this toward us. For their part they may be feeling that our specialness or overimportance makes everything, the relationship and family, revolve around us. On the other hand it could be us doing the attacking, because we feel unimportant next to our partner. Resentment bred from need and inequality can sour a relationship. This is when it is most important to commit to equality.

When a couple works their way through the power struggle and deadness stages of relationship and reach partnership, they have done so by joining in love thousands of times. They have accomplished this because at some point they committed to their equality which always brings about love. This re-establishes the lost bonding and by the time a couple reaches partnership, they have healed most of the competition, reached a balance of their masculine and feminine sides and a more natural balance in their relationship and life. If a couple keeps joining in love they will reach stages of leadership, vision and mastery together and while each partner may demonstrate one stage more than the other, they typically move through the stages together. In mastery a new and greater level of balance is brought about as God comes into the relationship in a lived way. Most of the roles and false jobs are given up as more and more is put into God's hands. Life becomes much more simple and balanced. Most *doing* is let go of except where there is inspiration or guidance to realise *being*, which contains natural inclusion, bonding, abundance and love. This moves beyond our insecurity to the point where we place ourselves in the natural centre of our lives. In so doing we place others in the centre of their lives. We know that this is a much truer state because of the peace, joy, effectiveness, love, compassion and grace which we experience naturally.

Exercise

Reflect on how much balance there is in your life between work and play, work and family. Examine how much space you are taking up in your work, your relationships and your world. If you are taking up too much space, you are probably making up for one or both of your parents who didn't take their place in the family, or in some cases took too much. Whether you appear too big or too small in certain situations, you will feel in sacrifice and resentful sometimes for opposite reasons.

Now is the time to correct this through the healing method of centring. Where we have been off our centres we will typically find ourselves out of balance and in sacrifice in all areas of our lives. Where we lost our centres, devalued or over inflated ourselves and have negative emotions or grievances from unbonded families, our lives can be negatively patterned to set up obstacles and traps. Still we can only be stopped where we want to be stopped or where we would use it as an excuse.

1. In your work, relationships and life in the present, ask your higher mind to carry you back to your centre now. If you attain a state of peace, you know you have attained your centre and are approaching the experience of being. If you have not achieved a feeling of deep peace, ask to be carried back to a second centre. Again, feel the results. If you have not experienced a deep state of peace, ask to be carried to a third centre. Ask to be carried to as many centres as you need to reach a state of deep peace. Continue this until you feel deeply connected and happy once more.

2. Now ask yourself intuitively when you first lost your centre as a child. Ask your higher mind to carry you and whoever was present back to your centres. Repeat this until you experience deep peace both emotionally and imaginatively. Some people like to be carried to as many centres as it takes them to turn the whole scene into light.

3. In any imbalance, in any problem with your relationship and family, put it all in the hands of God. Let it be balanced for you. Ask for the help or the miracles necessary to have this done. Let your work be done for you by grace. Learn to listen to your guidance. Let go of tasks that are not what you are called to do.

WAY 36 The World Is Our Dream

Buddhism states that the world is our dream and that we are asleep until we reach enlightenment, which is a realisation or awakening. The book of Genesis says that Adam fell into a deep sleep just before Eve was brought forth, yet nowhere does it say he ever woke up.

As a young therapist I studied, discovered and used a wide range of healing techniques for dreams. Dreams reflect hidden wishes, sometimes many conflicting wishes jumbled together. Our waking dream, the dream of life, and what we experience is no different, in that it reflects our wishes and our conflicting wishes. I have found that the experience or dream of everyday life lends itself to healing, using the same methods I found when I worked with dreams.

Let us look at any given day of our lives and the wealth of things which happen to us, and then imagine that each thing we do or each experience we have comes to us from our wishes. Even if it has negative consequences, we could ask ourselves what our wish could possibly have been that would bring such an event about in our lives. We could begin to examine fruitfully why we would do such a thing to ourselves and how this could possibly serve us. If we have done the exercise of Way 24 properly, we have first hand experience of the tangled ball of wishes within us and how some of these wishes not only go against our conscious mind but also can be very dark. Freud once described dreams as the royal road to the unconscious. And dreams, whether they are waking or sleeping, can help us to discover our unconscious motivations. If we look with the eyes of awareness, we can see that everyday life is also a royal road to the unconscious. As we further see our world as a dream, we realise that the only expedient way to transform our dreams is through changing ourselves as the dreamer. If we regard our lives and experiences as the dreams our wishes have made, a way emerges for us to become aware of ourselves and our unconscious wishes. If we wanted to change a movie in a theatre we wouldn't go up and try to change the image on the screen, we would go back to the projector. In this case the projector is ourselves and we can get to the heart of any issues in our lives by going back to the wishes where our dreams are made, our own private Hollywood – the ego. It is full of idle wishes like, 'I wonder what would happen if . . .' This type of curiosity can have disastrous consequences at times.

At some point in our dreaming we might realise that we are dreaming and then become interested in awakening. We may all have done this in the throes of a nightmare. And if we ever follow our thoughts for a while we realise that we and everyone, even the most successful people, don't fully value ourselves, attack ourselves and even throw ourselves away at times. This is obviously a mistake, but one which needs our conscious awareness if our thoughts and willingness are to let it all go and move in a positive direction.

We could begin by asking what we thought the wish under each experience would get for us. Sometimes it is helpful to ask this question a number of times to get all the reasons which might be present in any given situation. As an example, here is a typical instance of someone having an accident and what the wishes could have been. It is important to remember these are just a few of the thousands of answers which can come up.

What was I trying to get by my accident today?
Suffering
What am I trying to get by my suffering from this accident?
Sacrifice
What am I trying to get by my sacrifice?
I am trying to save my mother

Of course, we may find that this accident has just the opposite effect of what we wished. Instead of saving our mother it might, for instance, give her a heart attack. Our ego strategies do work at times but they never succeed in making us happy and they set us up in impossible situations. Happiness comes from love, joining and the success of partnership, which is the opposite of the ego as separation, competition and specialness.

Too many of us are dreaming nightmares and it makes for a nightmare world. Many of our wishes are based on agendas which we would readily release if we examined them consciously. It is not uncommon to think a hundred thoughts a minute. How many of them are we aware of? We can make split-second decisions and as a result of these many thoughts we are only half-aware of what we are doing before we immediately repress it.

Monsters and bad guys in our sleeping dreams are shadow figures, parts of our mind we've judged, split off and repressed as bad. They all seem to be out to get us in our dreams but ultimately they just want to join us again. A dream is full of our self-concepts. The waking dream of our everyday life portrays people who are shadow figures to us and our shadow self-concepts. Shadow figures in the news are shadow figures from the collective unconscious, though what is a shadow figure in one part of the world can be a hero in another part of the world. The world is both our personal and our collective dream but if one person changed the dream at a significant depth of the unconscious, it could change it for everyone. If we are willing to consider healing at this level we have an opportunity to do so by looking at the world through healing eyes.

Sometimes we unconsciously attack ourselves

first, before we project on the people around us who we then judge and attack. The fact that the self-attack is unconscious seems to our ego to make it safe to project, judge and attack those outside us. Forgiveness and self-forgiveness are such important healing principles because in self-forgiveness we also forgive the world and when we forgive the world we are also released and know ourselves as innocent in the same way.

Let us consider the types of dreams that we've been dreaming in our daily lives. Are these heart-breaks or dreams of war? Do we live in dreams of guilt, revenge or sacrifice? Are there fear, scarcity or tragic dreams? Do we have dreams of control, sacri-fice or soap operas? Or do we have happy, healing, loving and romantic dreams? Are your life dreams boring or full of adventure? Do you have success-with-ease types of dreams, or hard work dreams and against-all-odds-and-difficulties types of dreams? Are your dreams beautiful, heroic or carefree? If you choose happy dreams rather than dark dreams, it is much easier to awaken and bring about the end of all dreams. We will have many awakenings to free us from bad dreams and our final awakening and enlightenment will be to love, light, spirit, and one-ness.

Exercise

- Reflect on your life and the kinds of dreams you have.

- Make a list of them. Ask yourself how many of each of these dreams you have, especially the negative ones?
- If you are willing, imagine yourself placing each of these negative waking dreams in God's hands.
- See and feel what you are given back to replace such bad dreams both for yourself and for the world.

WAY 37 From Specialness to Love

When bonding is lost, competition begins. The ego is always out to win over others. It will even feed on dark glamour and losses, so it will have the most loss or suffering, feasting on the recognition that results. Our ego has as much need for specialness as we have for love. To the extent that we have love, there is no need for specialness. The ego wants to make its mark and be known for some achievement even if it's dubious. Of course, this sets it in conflict with the part of the ego that wants us to hide. If the ego is not exaggerating itself in grandiosity, it then wants to be as small as possible. The specialness which the ego wants for itself distracts and subverts us from the specialness of our purpose, that which we promised at a soul level we would accomplish for the world. Happiness and fulfilment come to us as a result of our love, our giving and forgiving and completing our life's purpose.

Until we realise the difference between specialness and love, our lives can be one long, interminable competition to get attention and feed our insatiable ego. We don't realise that this is one of the fundamental reasons our relationships don't work out. We get caught in the vicious circle of superiority-inferiority, driven by specialness, which the ego uses to stop the healing, joining and happiness generated through bonding. Specialness becomes a goal that leads to separation and inequality. Specialness, which is counterfeit love, is built on narcissism and compensation for feelings of inadequacy, and it leads to all the fights, competition and deadness in relationships. It is what the ego uses to subvert and sabotage our relationships, since as the principle of separation it is completely inept at intimacy. Most people confuse love, the principle of sharing and inclusion, with specialness, the principle of getting and separation, in spite of the fact that love builds and specialness holds others hostage to our needs. Once we begin to discern the difference between specialness and true relatedness, we can really begin to leap forward in relationships.

Specialness is a key element in problems, not only because of its desire to take something, but also because whatever comes to it is never enough. The 'taking' or 'getting' of specialness leads to devaluing ourselves and others, because what we take we don't value. Specialness brings about hurt and loneliness since people pull away from us as we try to take from them, even when it's under the disguise of giving. Specialness is a compensation for feelings of neediness and not being enough, which block our ability to receive. This means it comes about through lost bonding and separation. This type of ego behaviour not only stops appreciation and gratitude from others, it generally blocks love, success and abundance because it is investing only in itself. In our effort to 'get' the world to revolve around us, we turn others into objects as tribute to our ego. But when we objectify others we do the same to ourselves so that we become dissociated and unable to receive and enjoy. Specialness wants to be king of the world. Specialness wants to knock God off His throne and take over. Specialness could gain the whole world and lose sight of its soul and what's important. Specialness could gain the whole world and not enjoy it. Specialness could gain the whole world and it still wouldn't be enough. Specialness could live a shallow, selfish, soul-less existence and not know it.

Exercise

Make a list of past major problems or heartbreaks you have suffered. Examine each one to see where your need for specialness was generating the problem. The awareness that comes about is a key aspect in preventing you from making poor investments again. You may want to apologise to others and forgive yourself as a result of these past mistakes. It will certainly make it easier to be accountable for your life experience and forgive others when you realise that when you thought others were victimising you, you were using the situation to become separate and special.

Now make a list of current problems and look for the hidden or not so hidden need for specialness in them. Recognise that your plan of having a present problem in order to be special is actually generating suffering not only for yourself but for the others who are being used. This does not make for love; it builds resentment.

Imagine now that you took one of your current problems, recognising your attempt and your desire for specialness. Imagine yourself letting go of the specialness and choosing love instead. Sit quietly and listen within to how you can bring about and give love instead of trying to be special. As you feel and give love, it opens you to receive love and natural appreciation from those around you.

Problem	The way I was trying to be Special	What kind of Specialness did I want?

Go through each need for specialness and let yourself be inspired with how you could give love in that experience instead.

Ask yourself intuitively, how old you were when this specific need for specialness began? Did it ever work to be special? Did it ever satisfy your need, or make you happy?

Now in this original situation, imagine yourself giving love to make things better.

WAY 38   Healing Proofs and Self-Concepts

In every problem we have set out to prove something. Most of the time we attempt to prove positive things about ourselves and less positive things about others, keeping our superiority. However, we wouldn't need to prove them unless we didn't really believe them. This kind of proving goes into demonstrating to others what good, hardworking, worthy and loveable people we are. We expend vast amounts of energy and have many problems to support these positive self-concepts. An example may be, 'I must be a good person, look at how I suffer, how hard I work, what I put up with . . .' In spite of all the energy we expend, proving does not allow receiving because the negative self-concept hides what we really believe about ourselves. All of the positive response or reward goes to the compensating self-concept to support it; what little we ourselves might receive in this way is quickly exhausted by the sacrifice required by the proving. In rarer cases we seek to prove negative things about ourselves. The purpose of this is to hide our true goodness, our innocence, power and radiance that exists at the *being* or mastery level of our minds.

All of these positive, compensatory self-concepts keep us stuck as the result of our split-mind. We act nice, but feel exhausted, uninvolved, depressed, dead or burned out. Their main purpose is to hide the corresponding opposite, dark and negative shadow self-concepts buried inside. It also explains why bad things happen to good people because, at some level, we believe we are bad and deserving of punishment even though we act so good. In keeping the unconscious repressed, we attempt to defer the punishment of our guilt. We punish ourselves so that God needn't bother. All these negative self-concepts are, for the most part, hidden from us under denial and self-deception. There is a strong reaction and compensation against any such negative quality. We judge and repress it and then project it out to someone in the world, and condemn them in an attempt to separate ourselves from them because we think we are better.

Yet not only are shadow figures or negative self-concepts compensated for by 'good' roles, they are themselves a compensation. At some fundamental level the purpose of these negative self-concepts is to prove that we are actually bad, evil and nasty as a way of hiding our true goodness, power and connection to grace – our higher mind and holiness which we seem even more frightened of embracing. To the ego this level is positively terrifying because it demonstrates to us that we do not need our ego. Therefore the ego is invested in a slow down so we don't get past our compensating 'good' roles and we don't examine and recognise that our beliefs that we are bad, evil and nasty are spurious and just meant to keep us from evolving.

Beliefs make up our perceptions of the world and every belief comes from a self-concept. For instance, if we believe the world is painful, uncaring and hard, at some level we will believe that we are painful, uncaring and hard, even though we may act in an opposite way. This would be a compensation to protect ourselves or hide against judgement even though we've already judged ourselves.

Self-concepts generate what we see in our perception as we look at the mirror of the world. Our self-concepts are the glasses through which we peer at the world. To forgive the world is to forgive ourselves, thus making both benign.

All of our self-concepts and beliefs keep us from seeing rightly. As we keep evolving, and especially as we begin to evolve beyond independence to interdependence, we naturally begin to let go of unsuccessful beliefs and self-concepts. As we reach interdependence we begin to let go of shadow self-concepts and dark beliefs and finally all beliefs and self-concepts, so that right perception, true discernment and grace guide us. Finally as we reach the state of radical dependence or realising ourselves as a child of God, we open ourselves to spiritual knowledge and the *being* levels of the mind, moving past perception altogether.

Each situation we are in, each problem we have, is a sign of negative beliefs and self-concepts. The ego uses problems as a defence because without them we would realise our true goodness, which is beyond the dictates of the ego. Here the ego feels so threatened that it is willing to keep us imprisoned with problems and traps to protect itself from being judged as unnecessary; this would happen once we realised ourselves as radically dependent on God as our loving parent and without the need to do everything, even anything, ourselves.

The defences the ego uses to hide negative beliefs and self-concepts are denial and repression. This keeps us unaware of how beliefs are the underpinning of perception and thus experience. All beliefs and self-concepts are based on judgement which, of course, sets up distance, separation and thus, the ego. Eventually, in interdependence, we realise that even our positive beliefs and self-concepts are blocking something greater – a spiritual reality not dictated or established by us, which we can reach to once more as we let go of our self-concepts.

Letting go of a belief or self-concept once we realise it is there is a very easy way of moving beyond it and on to the next step. Simply choosing that we will no longer invest in it could heal a self-concept. Typically in this world we begin by building a strong character and ego, then later in our further evolution toward mastery, we begin to let go and integrate our personalities, which are our self-concepts. This means there is less and less of our ego, and all of its frenzied doing, and more peace for grace and heaven to pour through.

In letting go of self-concepts, like beliefs, it is important to realise that there may be many layers of beliefs and personalities. Each choice or letting go we make can dislodge and then open up another one. When there is a strong realisation of the futility of certain self-concepts, a whole pattern, which may previously have run our lives, can be released. Alternatively, we could simply make a choice to let go of each of the self-concepts we are trying to prove and instead replace them with new choices that reflect the truth of our goodness. As we do so we begin slowly but surely to see ourselves as God sees us. We will uncover not only repressed pockets of very dark self-concepts but also transcendent parts of the mind, which the ego has indiscriminately repressed as threatening. We will then find our true beauty and goodness, power and will as established by God. We can begin to give up our pockets of insanity and self-hatred. As we clear our fear and ego-invested beliefs and self-concepts we evolve into the wholeness and grace of our being.

We can stop investing in these self-concepts now. We can choose to let them go and ask for the truth. This would give us the miracle mindedness to allow for heaven's solution. God as our Father always has a way through for us if we would not be too frightened and allow it.

Exercise

1. Ask yourself:

- *The positive things I am trying to prove about myself by having this problem are . . .*
- *The negative things I am trying to prove about myself are . . .*
- *The negative things I am trying to prove about the*

situation or life in general by having this problem are . . .

- *The person I am trying to prove negative things about by having this problem is . . .*
- *What I am trying to prove about them is . . .*

List all of the positive proofs as the roles and compensations that keep us split minded and in sacrifice. Now list all of the negative qualities which the problem proves. Recognise these dark self-concepts and the judgements you have on others are all your own self-concepts, which you support with time, energy and money, but from which you are unable to receive.

Problem	Positive Compensating Self-Concepts	Negative Compensating Self-Concepts

Make the choice to let all of these self-concepts go as beliefs which limit you and are unnecessary for your happiness and well being.

2. *I believe that life is* _____,
_____ *and* _____.

I believe that I am _____,
_____ *and* _____.

I believe the world is _____,
_____ *and* _____.

I believe my partner is _____,
_____ *and* _____.

I believe my ex-partner is _____,
_____ *and* _____.

I believe my worst enemy is _____,
_____ *and* _____.

I believe money is _____,
_____ *and* _____.

I believe sex is _____,
_____ *and* _____.

I believe success is _____,
_____ *and* _____.

I believe true love is _____,
_____ *and* _____.

I believe my life is _____,
_____ *and* _____.

My worst experience was _____,
_____ *and* _____.

Recognise that all of these answers are actually
self-concepts. Put them all in the hands of your
higher mind, category by category. Ask your
higher mind to replace them with something
of greater value.

Taking the Next Step on the Path to Our Purpose

Whenever we have a problem, especially a chronic problem, we are using it to avoid our purpose. Every problem contains within it the fear of the next step and our fear of going forward, and reflects our lack of willingness to change and live our purpose. Yet the next step contains within it a new level of confidence, success, purpose and intimacy. Willingness naturally brings the next step in our lives to us. The will to go forward frees our lives and makes living easier. Although the next step naturally makes our lives better, we would already be there if we were not frightened of it. We think we would lose something, or have to give up some hidden or not so hidden indulgence or attachment to have our lives unfold. Somehow we don't feel adequate or deserving of the next step. But this is not true, it's merely how our ego scares us from moving forward. The next step is a true level of progress, a new step in development in which we follow the path already designed for us. This is a step toward our purpose, what we are called to give and our destiny of who we came to be. This path is the easiest and most carefree way for us to evolve and become ourselves in order to reach our being, love, creativity and happiness. Few of us take this path because we feel we have a better idea about how to run our lives. We believe our ultimate freedom is to design and live our own lives. This attitude generates great hardship and much sacrifice and it is possible to become lost in our problems, completely distracted from what life is about and what we promised to contribute to it. Our attempt to do it all ourselves is full of rebellion and revenge against heaven and our true selves and it is a way of not getting the job done or only with great difficulty. Deeper in our minds it becomes evident that this attitude is generated by the authority conflict, which is full of dissociated independence, rebellion and revenge against our parents and God. Sacrifice and the roles and rules, though they seem to be the opposite of rebellion and dissociated independence, actually lead to it and become just another way to witness the separation and resist grace.

If we are not completely consumed and delayed by our problems then we find some other way to distract ourselves from the fear of our purpose. Problems, distractions, detours and delay are prominent weapons of the ego, which uses them as a way to continue and strengthen its existence. Simply taking the next step is one easy way to melt a layer of the ego and the separation made by fear.

We don't actually take a step forward. We choose the next step and it comes to us allowing us more partnership and grace. Most of us are half asleep, acting like good-nice-dead people, thinking we would never rebel or take revenge, but we hide those elements from ourselves and compensate for them.

Giving up rules, compensations and what we hide from ourselves does not mean giving up acting civilised or having good manners. It does mean being authentic, aware, real and more truly ethical because we are not playing out the hundreds of deadening roles, which are only compensations leading to burnout. Our roles are compensating self-concepts meant to hide feelings of failure from painful, unhealed experiences of the past. Roles are ways we behave to be nice while trying to make up for guilt and failure, but they are just another trap to delay us. In roles we wear ourselves out doing what we are not called to do in an ineffective way, and so we don't complete what it is we have come to do. We are using these distractions so as not to face the fear and do what we are truly called to do, which is the only thing that would fulfil us and make us happy. To embrace our purpose is to clear up most of our problems and the conspiracies we've set up as an excuse. The only ones remaining would be those specifically needed for our purpose. To live our purpose is a giant leap forward in our lives and it brings much ease and fulfilment.

Our true life path is already set up for us. It is within us but we are afraid to know it fully. Sometimes out of fear we really get off our true path, as indicated by how painful things are in our lives. Yet even so a detour can turn into a natural part of our path. Every step of the way is shown for us if we would only listen within for guidance. We need not be frightened of our purpose. We don't have to fall for the ego's trap of thinking we have

to do it all ourselves. No matter how big our purpose is, we will be helped by those around us and
by grace which will accomplish it through us. Many
times the sheer amount of work necessary to complete our purpose can be daunting. At some level
the amount of work we feel *we* have to do is a misinterpretation, which is generated from the present
roles and sacrifice that we are in. We mistakenly
believe that we would have to give up even more of
our lives and sacrifice even more of ourselves.
Strangely, we begin to believe that our purpose
would be an act of sacrifice, in which we would
either not be true to ourselves, or have to give up
our personal life to accomplish a greater good for
the world. This sets up a powerful conspiracy against
our purpose from which only truth frees us. Yet our
purpose is our true path and can only be accomplished by being true to ourselves. Our fear that we
are too small to accomplish our purpose has at times
been reinforced by our parents, families, teachers,
friends and ourselves. Yet those outside us represent
our subconscious, projected doubts. This sets up
conflict, which makes us not only want to hide from
the amount of work we are called to handle, but
also fear that we'd lose our chance for personal
happiness. By not facing this mistake, we hide from
our purpose and seek to divert ourselves in the world
by merely making money or trying to pleasure ourselves. Yet we are called for transcendence and to
contribute something greater which would bring
happiness to others and ourselves. There is a way
out of every conspiracy including this one, if there

is the will. Our desire to accomplish our purpose can melt through every trap, misstep and conspiracy. Our will to find the way brings the next step to us. Our willingness cuts through our fear and mis-interpretations and brings the truth of our pathway home. After any initial confusion which might come as a result of changing course, the pull and attraction of what we have come to give the world out of our love becomes stronger and stronger with each step.

Exercise

1. One way to check how much you are living your purpose is to ask yourself:

- *On the scale of 100 percent, how fulfilled am I in my life . . . ?*
- *How much do I feel I am living my purpose?*
- *What delays or distractions are there in my life?*

There is a direct correlation between how ful-filled you feel and how much you are living your purpose. Notice what you may be using to hold yourself back from your purpose. What roles or duties are you using to keep yourself from moving forward through your heaviness, hard work, inability to receive or burnout? What problems are you using to stop yourself, to hold yourself back? Is there an emotion you are using, such as fear, guilt, heartbreak, sadness and depression to stop yourself? They can only hold you back if you want them to. You can make another choice.

Become aware of the work you are called to do today. If long-term projects are weighing on you, then reflect on them for a moment. In spite of whatever seems to be holding you back, choose to be free of it as many times as necessary to counter any trap or stoppage.

2. Imagine yourself putting all your jobs, work, projects, fear and heaviness into the hands of God. Today do this until you achieve a sense of being carefree. Keep putting everything in God's hands until you feel the peace and centredness within you. This allows grace to pass through you to accomplish whatever task is at hand.

3. Choose to take the next step. This occurs by doing the next thing there is to do, but also by being willing to have the next step occur. This has the effect of bringing either the next step in growth to you or bringing you to a new level of progress. Know that it is your true desire to give yourself and your love, and to know yourself in the giving, which leads you to your purpose. How much you want your purpose with your whole heart is how much you'll have it.

WAY 40 The Family Conspiracy and Its Origins

The extent to which our families weren't bonded brought about deep-seated feelings of failure, guilt and valuelessness, which were at times so strong that we threw ourselves away and haven't recovered since. Even less traumatic loss of bonding sets up patterns of competition, dissociation, independence, sacrifice, fusion and dependency as well as feelings of guilt, failure and valuelessness. From valuelessness comes deep caches of unworthiness, death temptations or the roles to cover it all up. Many problems emerge from this deep layer of family guilt, failure and valuelessness, not the least of which are ineffectiveness, busyness, inability to receive and shadow figures (which is self-attack and projecting our negative self-beliefs on those around us).

Valuelessness, then, comes from chronic family issues which have become patterns in our lives and give rise to both relationship and victim issues. Our valuelessness and major family issues all come from the unconscious. These are soul level and ancestral issues, which we brought into this life to learn, resolve and undo. Valuelessness comes from our deepest experiences of failure and when this feeling emerges we are tempted to die, which is why we use most of what we do, our 'doingness', as a form of compensation to hide it. However, it is ineffective because we don't receive for what we do because we use it as a defence. This makes for a lot of wasted time and effort in life.

We experienced this failure in childhood when we felt we failed our family: we felt we were not able to save the family or a family member from their pain or problem. As a result we inherited their pain which we typically cover over with grievances. Whenever we have grievances from our past it's because we inherited someone's pain which caused them to act in some way, which brought about the same pain in them or those around them. Our inherited pain was then covered over by judgement, grievances and further overlaid by defences of dissociation, repression, compensation of roles, busyness and doing.

The evidence that our family was bonded is the presence of love, co-operation, success, ease, health, the joy of being together as well as few and minor problems. If this is the case, we have felt only minor guilt, shame or competition and are probably working on mostly spiritual issues in our lives. Having met and heard of tens of thousands of families around the world, I have heard of only one family that might have been bonded. But since this report came from someone who was interviewing me long distance I couldn't confirm it. This is just to put in perspective how rare a fully bonded family is and that dysfunction is the norm. I see some evidence of a whole new level of bonded families emerging now but they still have to deal with any dysfunction in their original families that's being passed down to them and their spouses. What isn't healed is passed down.

Our family pattern is one of the greatest influences, if not the greatest influence, in our lives and for the most part it is completely subconscious. Yet our family pattern sets up our relationship pattern. It is our family and relationship patterns which set up our success, failure or victim patterns. The misunderstandings can be so profound in childhood around our parents and family that they can affect our confidence, belief systems, emotions and experiences in whole areas of our lives. The subconscious mind is seemingly so complicated that it is a rare individual who, through some form of healing, resolve or giving, is able to surmount or transcend the family pattern. It was only after eighteen years of work that I felt I finally understood the subconscious. After thirty years of studying the mind and human experience this naturally has refined and I've gone on to study the unconscious and now the super conscious. But only after I had come to understand family dynamics did I feel that my understanding of the subconscious mind was complete. The trap the ego sets up around our family dynamics is so profound that the family conspiracy, a trap so strong that it is set up to never be got through, cripples us emotionally, hides our purpose and keeps us diminished and unaware of our greatness.

Yet, as with any conspiracy, there are simple and profound ways to clear a layer of it or collapse it altogether. The family conspiracy and the Oedipal

Conspiracy (which we will examine in Way 42) are so primordial and interwoven in our minds that usually we heal layer after layer of these same conspiracies as we evolve.

The extent to which we have grievances, were hurt, victimised or any of the family had problems, was the extent to which we felt and still feel guilty as a result of what we see as our failure to help or even save them. Basically we inherited from our families the very pain we came to heal. The bonding from our childhood is a measure of how much we succeeded in our soul's agenda with our families.

Our souls have a certain agenda that is expressed interpersonally in our family. Our families are not an accidental or random assignation but purposeful in that the lessons we need for our purpose are, for the most part, present in our original families. Once we learn that we have the very gifts within us waiting to be given to our families to save them from their pain, we have taken a giant step in healing the family conspiracy. It is these very gifts which we have come to give the world through our purpose.

At an unconscious level the family is a mirror of the parts of our mind which we have judged and projected but which in this life we came to re-integrate, thus healing the pain and mutually sharing the gifts we each brought in. The family represents the deepest unconscious parts which we need for our purpose.

The extent to which we succeed in bonding with them and resolving the problems is the extent of how much the blueprint for our purpose we have developed and realised. For instance, if we can succeed with mother or father, there is no one with whom we will not succeed in helping in this very area. Where we don't succeed in the family, guilt, failure, suffering and valuelessness spring up. When we feel valueless we feel like we want to die.

The ego attempts to protect us from this by compensation, doingness and repetition compulsion, which is feeling driven to repeat things even if they don't succeed. All of our doing, unless inspired, comes from this. All of this, including our roles and compensations, are what we use to cover the original guilt, failure and valuelessness.

What this ego strategy succeeded in doing was to move us out of our centres where we could have restored the bonding easily through grace. As we left our centres of grace, peace and innocence, we came into sacrifice, hard work, busyness, difficulty, fusion problems and attempting to play a 'good' role, which is an attempt to make up for the soul level injury and guilt which shows up as family issues and fractures. Of course, compensation never succeeds in atoning for the guilt and the family issues which repeat our soul patterns, set up our whole psychology and all that needs to be healed in us. The family guilt and its ensuing valuelessness are typically so buried under further relationship and victim patterns that it is a wonder anyone can free themselves and reach, once again, this level of being, innocence, grace and wholeness. As we clear the family conspiracy we begin to experience our being and wholeness; we once again begin to remember

God. This shifts our consciousness from 'doing' to 'being' and it sets up a fundamental change to true perception. In the state of being, we accomplish and do everything first by guidance or inspiration and then by grace.

There are four major layers of guilt in the mind and each one has great impact in our lives. While guilt in any form leads to conflict, being stuck, fear, self-attack, suffering, destruction, and even death, clearing a major layer of it has great healing effect and raises us up to a new level of success. Using compensation to try to avert guilt's destructiveness is ineffective, because it merely covers over the issue but doesn't significantly move us forward. All are attempts to separate us from the guilt which we are experiencing. Our defences, of course, don't really work and the amount of our doing, judgement and sacrifice (giving without receiving or giving without inspiration or guidance as a form of delay) speaks of the amount of guilt we all have which we try our best to deny. The four layers of guilt are: 1) the everyday layer which contains what we felt we did wrong and what we felt we didn't do right; 2) where we felt we failed in our original family; 3) guilt coming from ancestral and soul patterns; and 4) where we experience ourselves as separated from God. The root of all guilt comes from this third layer.

To free ourselves from the trap of valuelessness, guilt and failure in our family would be quite remarkable because it would mean that we had healed most of the first layer of guilt, what we felt we did wrong or didn't do right. Besides this there is the original guilt of separation, which underlies our family patterns and stacks the cards against us in healing family guilt. Because even when you heal a family trauma, if there is more guilt coming from soul or ancestral patterns or from the separation from God then these incidents will fill up with more primordial guilt until the root situation is resolved. One of the core hidden intentions for the failures we experienced in our family is that as we become more guilty, we also get to be more independent and dissociated. These are two of the things the ego, the principle of separation, is made out of because the extent to which there is separation, there is fear and guilt.

We come into the family to help, heal and save it. The dynamics of our families and its members seem so big, that we fall into an age old pattern and trap of leaving our being, our centres of peace and grace in an attempt to reach out and save our family members. This pattern, which already exists at a soul level and is re-enacted in our families, leads to sacrifice on our part and greater degrees of fusion; it contains the muddling of individual boundaries and sacrifice, so we feel we are carrying this person and our families on our backs. This is a mistaken general tendency to try to help through roles and sacrifice, which is both ineffective and uncalled for in the sense that through our roles and sacrifice, we actually use the person or situation to hold us back rather than really move forward. In the muddled boundaries between us, every time a family member feels pain, we suffer accordingly. It makes it exceptionally hard to heal pain that we are suffering from, which isn't really ours as such. This fusion or untrue joining is the ego's best counterfeit answer to bonding. It includes sacrifice that merely covers over the guilt we experience for not saving this family member. We feel separation and failure, which actually stems from our primordial guilt feelings passed down ancestrally, negative soul patterns and of separation from oneness. All of this comes between us and family members. This dynamic of failure in the family is so strong that the trap of not being able to save others becomes a conspiracy against ourselves and our purpose. So many of us have failed to help, much less save our families, that common wisdom in the counselling community in the United States is to not even try to save the family. Of course, this advice doesn't take into consideration that we all feel impelled to save our families and that our families contain the blueprint of the lessons to be learned, and gifts to be realised, to restore our families to bonding and for us to realise our purpose.

Our purpose is tied in with our family dynamics. The problem about failure is that we try to do it ourselves. We fall into sacrifice, fusion, resentment and burnout. If we were to invoke grace, we could meet the challenge, retain our centre and our being, keep or restore the bonding and give the soul level gift necessary to free our family. I've yet to find someone who didn't fall into this trap as a child. If someone had not done so they would be at a mastery level consciousness. As it is we left or fell out of being and into doing, sentencing ourselves to a life of sacrifice and compensation without the ability to receive. This leads from our roles of sacrifice to burnout and roles of independence, which keep us busy. In other words we're all 'doing time'.

If we followed the advice of the counselling community and did not try to save the family, even if it were possible to save us from the fusion-sacrifice-guilt, it would just lead to a state of dissociation and independence which is just a compensation for guilt. Of course, most us end up dissociated anyway after trying to save the family through sacrifice and then burning out. This then is the family conspiracy, a trap set up so well it looks like it can never be got out of, leaving our centres to attempt to save the family and falling into fusion, sacrifice and roles leading to burnout and dissociated independence. This can be resolved through the re-establishment of bonding. Acts of love, joining, forgiveness, helping, giving, appreciating, sharing and centring can make a major difference. Also the centring method, which returns the family, layer by layer back to its place of love, peace, grace, balance and bonding, has the effect of transforming and re-establishing the bonding which is lost through trauma (problems coming from the family from ancestors) or from a soul level. Through giving the soul level gifts which we have brought in to help our family and its members, bonding is also restored and chronic problems fall away. For the most part at this point in our lives these gifts are buried under pain and grievances. We end up, typically, inheriting the wounds of our parents and either live them out or suffer them under our compensations. But once we recognise the principles involved it is not difficult to find the gifts, free our parents or family of the trap through our gifts and pass it up through the family, thus freeing our ancestors of these karmic patterns. This can be done layer by layer all the while freeing ourselves, our partners and our families.

It is the family problem patterns that set up our relationship problem patterns and it is our relationship problem patterns that set up our victim patterns. All of these are set up by soul patterns, what we have come to learn and heal and, of course, from that original guilt pattern of separation from God. So the family conspiracy and its resolution has a lot to do with our success in relations and career, living our purpose and embracing our destiny. Given what there is to heal, it's a wonder any of us finds a way through into true love, leadership, vision and mastery. To fully resolve the family guilt and the valuelessness which comes from it, we need to reach a level of bonding with our present and original family. To accomplish this we would naturally have reached the mastery level of consciousness. Of course, there are many traps and conspiracies even before we get to the family conspiracy. As we reach mastery we will once again realise our being and eschew doing except as guided. In the success of healing the family conspiracy or second layer of guilt we address soul and ancestral issues and begin to desire oneness and to address resolution of the guilt of the last or spiritual layer. The wholeness, or being which we would experience in healing the family conspiracy, would lead to the experience of wholeness and the remembrance of God. Accomplishing this wholeness takes a true dedication to healing, evolution and later the desire for realisation and enlightenment. Healing the seemingly impossible layer of family guilt and its compensations lets us know that this and many other chronic problems can be undone and that there is a way through, in spite of the traps and conspiracies.

Exercise

Centring and giving the gifts of our souls which we brought in to heal the family are two of the major ways to heal the loss of bonding, sacrifice, fusion and dissociated patterns that began or were replayed in family situations. The following exercises use the healing methods of centring and gift-giving to resolve the problem.

1. Choose a family trauma or the moment an issue began. Ask your higher mind to carry everyone in your problem situation there back to their centres, that place of peace and innocence inside where you can receive grace. Having made this request, just relax. Notice how you feel. It is at times necessary to ask to be carried back to more centres until you reach a place of deep peace and light, especially regarding traumas. At your request your higher mind will take you and whoever is in the situation, back to as many

centres inside you as is necessary to succeed
with this exercise. After each request notice how
the peace has increased. Then once again ask
to be returned to the next centre. Some people
like to keep asking until the original scene has
turned to pure light and they're feeling the experience of joy.

2. Now ask to be carried back to where the root
of this problem began and again repeat the
centring exercise.

3. Now imagine yourself back at the time of a
painful event in your family, look inside those
around you. What is it they need? Imagine yourself opening the doors of your mind, heart and
soul and giving them this most needed and
most precious gift. This frees you and them
from the old family patterns, rewrites present
scripts, resolves the problem and opens a new
level of giftedness and freedom for everyone
involved.

WAY 41 The Fear Underneath

As we saw in Way 2, any problem we have has been generated by fear. Whenever there is a negative situation of any kind, there is fear underneath – a fear that generates the problem, and a fear which comes from our judgement of the problem and our resistance to it. This resistance or judgement compounds our original fear. The more fear we have the more we become paralysed and unable to move forward with our lives. If we become aware of the fear underneath, if we heal it or make another decision, then we can make progress, especially because we are now dealing with the root of the issue. As we heal the root fear then we and the situation begin to unfold in such a way as to make ourselves available for inspiration and grace.

In any problem situation, as we let go of the fear of negative things occurring, we then get in touch with the fear of all of the positive things which can occur. This is both a more hidden and a more chronic fear. This may sound absurd or even crazy because we work so hard for positive things, but time and again I have seen that we fear having the exceptionally positive occur, as the more primordial fear. This is because we feel we lack the confidence to handle or sustain the really 'good stuff'. The list of positive things we are afraid of includes God, love, happiness, having it all, intimacy, sex, money, success, relationships; which come about as the result of the fear of loss, being overwhelmed, losing control or loss of self.

Exercise

Imagine how much you dislike the problem or negative situation you are now experiencing. Imagine that the judgement causing the problem was turned into linear space and that this actually becomes the physical space between you and the problem's resolution. Add to this all the fear the problem generates and the underlying fear that brought it about and turn this into linear space between you and resolution of the problem.

Imagine you are as many physical steps away from the situation as you would need to take to reach the problem and have it resolve itself. If you are in a physical space where you can actually put yourself as many steps away as it would take to heal this and act it out, so much the better.

Problem Resolution . . . . Self

Once you have placed yourself as many steps away as it would take to resolve the problem, ask yourself: *'The fear which is coming about as a result of the problem itself is . . . ?* 'Whatever pops into your mind choose to let it go. Then take a step forward. Now ask yourself, '*What I am really afraid of that hides under my judgement is . . .*' Whatever pops into your mind is that which is holding you back. When you are ready to no longer let it hold you back, declare: '*I choose to let this go and to step forward.*' Take a step forward. Keep repeating this question to yourself and taking steps forward until that question seems to have exhausted itself and be complete.

Keep asking this question until there seems to have no more energy or response to it. Then ask yourself, '*The fear I had that brought about this problem is . . . ?*' When something pops into your mind, again make the decision, '*I choose to let this go and step forward.*' Again when this question seems to have spent itself ask the next question. If your initial intuition was something like a thousand steps, you could just use general categories for each step so that you then might bring it down to 10 or 20 steps as you prefer, but choose a number of steps that are 'doable'.

Now begin to ask yourself the next question:

'*The reason I have this problem is because the good thing I'm afraid would happen is . . . ?*'

Whatever pops into your mind once again say, 'I choose to let go of this fear and step forward.'

Take another step forward.

With each step repeat the question until you feel only the positive attraction between you and your goal, and you have finally covered all of the distance of separation between you and the positive outcome to your problem. Imagine yourself embracing the resolution and celebrating.

WAY 42   Healing the Oedipus Conspiracy

The Oedipal Complex can be identified as that which keeps us distant from our partner by the loss of intimacy. This may show itself as conflict, rejection, revulsion, repulsion, boredom, deadness in feeling or sexuality, withdrawal, sexual dysfunction including impotence and frigidity. Fear, withdrawal from life or relationships, exaggerated conforming roles, inauthenticity, sacrifice, feelings of failure and lack of protection are all signs of this Oedipal Complex. Incest, sexual abuse, sexual fantasies or dreams about sexual abuse in the family are also symptoms of the Oedipal Complex. Divorce, infidelity (of parents, self or partner) early sexualisation, pregnancy out of wedlock, sexual flirtatiousness that hides sexual repression, promiscuity or sexual dysfunction can all be signs of the Oedipal. Illness and death can also be examined for elements of oedipal withdrawal and self-punishment. The Oedipal can show up in your business or career as failure, excessive competition or lack of success.

The Oedipus Conspiracy is used by the ego to block or to stop altogether many of the good things of life. But the fact that it is, for the most part, not even conscious, keeps it effective as an ego trap. Most of all, by keeping relationships, which are our best chance for happiness, so muddled, confused or crippled, it keeps our ego strong while diverting us from our purpose.

The myths of our minds speak of the primordial ego patterns of our unconscious, which affect us at all levels. The most celebrated of these myths is that of Oedipus, made famous in Freud's theory of the Oedipal Complex, who killed his father and married his mother.

The myth of Oedipus begins with the prediction that the king's newborn son will kill him, so the king orders the baby to be killed. The new-born is placed on a hillside reserved for ill-formed babies and left to die. He is picked up by an old, childless couple who raise him. Oedipus eventually grows into a young man and he decides to make his way to the city to seek his fortune. As he travels, he is told to give way on the road by another man coming in the opposite direction. When he refuses, they struggle and the other is killed. Oedipus continues into the city and soon becomes quite popular. Within six months, since the king has disappeared, the queen decides to marry Oedipus. When all manner of plague and pestilence strike the country, Oedipus as the king seeks out the oracle, which tells him he has killed his father and married his mother. Horrified by the news, Oedipus blinds himself and wanders through Greece the rest of his days.

In classical psychology this story reflects a man's desire to kill his father and bed his mother, giving rise to all manner of guilt. This leads to fear of father's anger and castration, repression, and identification and fusion with the father as aggressor. It also brings about fear of power, success, intimacy and sex. In my work in the subconscious I have found this same mistaken pattern both in men and women and only rarely found evidence of the Electra complex, which is Freud's equivalent of the Oedipal Complex for women.

I began to see that symptoms of the Oedipal Complex were demonstrated by triangular relationships, dead relationships or no relationships. Sometimes even fighting in the relationship was also just a way of keeping distance from our partner, another oedipal symptom. I began to see that much of our guilt, sibling jealousy and anger, dilemmas, the madonna-whore syndrome, scarcity, competition, and our fear of sex, intimacy, success, and power are all part and parcel of this complex.

As symptoms of Oedipal Complex showed up in individuals and relationships when I worked as a marriage counsellor, I began to see how pervasive this complex is and how most of our relationship traps come from it. I noticed that it generates blocks in relationships, family, success, abundance, ease and intimacy. I saw evidence of it when people were stuck in drought having to do with relationships, feelings, sex, intimacy, romance, partnership or love in the relationship. In business there was evidence of it in failures, competition as a form of delay, sacrifice as an attempt to pay off guilt, fear of success and other forms of limitation. It was a prominent dynamic in affairs, triangles, lack of commitment, heartbreak both as a child and an adult, betrayals, jealousy, guilt and shame. I began to recognise that it was a key factor in about 85 percent of all relationship failures.

In 1984 I heard a dedicated young psychiatrist say, 'Come to my office five days a week, fifty weeks a year, from three to seven years and you may or may not be able to heal your Oedipal Complex.' This really bugged me because I knew that as sincere as this doctor was, if it was taking this long, there was something missing from our understanding. After another four years of concentrated study I began to realise not only how pervasive the Oedipal Complex was in relationships, I began to see the Oedipal Complex in the subconscious and unconscious. I could see that it was not just a pattern or a trap, but a conspiracy – a major trap so deftly put together that it seemed as if there was no way out. I realised for the first time that there were traps which the ego had set up not to be overcome, which I labelled 'conspiracies'. Specifically with regard to the Oedipal, the whole complex or conspiracy was subconscious so that most people didn't even know that it was there. With the help of the intuitive method I had developed years before to help people get in touch with what they had repressed, I could study people's experience of the Oedipal Conspiracy on my own without being bound by the limitations of Freud's theoretical model. I found a number of principles, methods and techniques, which helped people move through the diverse oedipal symptoms which they were experiencing. I found key elements in healing having to do with transforming conspiracies reconnecting the bonding in the family, centring and balancing the self, healing heartbreaking or incestuous relationships and balancing the family. I found that when the dysfunction in the family is healed, we complete a certain blueprint that helps us fulfil our purpose in the world. This opens us to the possibility of once again recommitting to our destiny and allows us to embrace our true self, giving up the pattern of sacrifice so ingrained in us.

Basically the Oedipus Conspiracy comes about from lack of bonding in our families. As a result we then experience distance, coldness, deprivation, fighting, heartbreak, the deadness which comes from fusion, affairs, dissociated independence, sacrifice and overburdening loyalties, uncommitted relationships, sexual abuse and so on. This lack of bonding is passed down to each generation, so unless we heal some of it, it's passed down to our children as we inherited it. When bonding is lost, a family loses its centre and as a result there are feelings of scarcity, inadequacy and competition for love. Sex loses its natural place as an expression of love and becomes either exaggerated or repressed. With bonding, sex is easily kept in perspective, naturally subsumed in love as one of its expressions. But, because of lack of bonding, as sexual attraction comes up it is taken out of proportion, which causes most family members to deal with it by repressing it, or exaggerating it by acting it out in sexual abuse or incest. Because of repression, most of us go around with this sexual attraction to family members buried deep inside of us. We then transfer onto our partners these hidden feelings, this unfinished business of guilt and sexual attraction toward our family members. As we turned away from these unresolved sexual attractions to family members, we also turn away from our partner whom we have transferred these feelings onto, bringing about emotional and sexual deadness with our partner.

Acting out the Oedipal Conspiracy, we find ourselves caught in triangle relationships or affairs which is the acting out of the original family pattern of competition, betrayal, and guilt. Sometimes we use heartbreaks or our own betrayal to pay off or hide evidence of our oedipal guilt. As a result of this unfinished oedipal guilt, we tend to shy away from success in relationships or career. Deadness, drought and dilemmas, of which the relationship triangles are the most dramatic examples, are also signs of an oedipal pattern at work. Dilemmas, which are the result of lost bonding, stem from the belief that we can't have mother's love and father's love equally. This may be especially evident in trying to choose between two partners but it can also show in a dilemma between work and family relationships or an imbalance in this area.

Also, when we get to the stage in our present relationship that we transfer the repressed sexual feeling from the family and project it on our partner, it easily leads to the end of sexual attraction. Sometimes when oedipal feelings are strong we even feel nauseous or repulsed by our partner. The Oedipal Conspiracy hides itself within, yet it drives, the common, contemporary experience of being too tired from a long days work at the office or with the children to even want to think about love, romance or sex with our partner.

In business, the Oedipal Conspiracy and the competition it engenders can lead to us becoming a 'shark', or on the other hand, being too afraid to succeed. If we were an oedipal winner, which means being closer to the parent of the opposite sex than our same sex parent was, we typically get what we want in life, but somehow can't receive or enjoy it. As oedipal losers, we don't allow ourselves to succeed in life because we would feel too guilty. Somehow we have the mistaken belief that success is tantamount to killing our same sex parent. Success for us in life, work and relationships is not an issue in a bonded family because the more bonding the more we can embrace love and success with ease.

So the Oedipal pattern is tied in with our whole family dynamic, and the lack of bonding passed down ancestrally. The more Oedipal Conspiracies we have had in our families, the more we will have the incumbent issues of sacrifice, competition, fusion, fear of the next step and fear of commitment. It is important to be aware of and heal oedipal issues through anything which brings about present bonding such as love, forgiveness, trust, commitment, joining, understanding and acceptance or letting go of guilt, attachments or pain.

The Oedipal Conspiracy which is a core family dynamic also has a corresponding pattern occurring at a spiritual level. Like family dynamics the Oedipal

Conspiracy has a pattern coming from that fourth or deepest layer of guilt. Here we find the mistaken beliefs that we have betrayed and killed God and stolen his gifts. Separation, which is the cause of the ego, is thus the cause of core guilt. This we project onto God making Him a god of condemnation, as if God Who is Love could ever do anything that wasn't pure Love. This sets up a separation pattern from the spiritual to the family level giving rise to both the Oedipal and Family Conspiracies. It also explains why these Oedipal Conspiracies are so difficult to heal: their roots are much deeper than the family. Whenever separation occurs on any level, the ego tells us that we have stolen their gifts and murdered them. This keeps us frightened on any level, but on the spiritual level it sets up an oedipal pattern with God.

The primordial separation and the primordial, but mistaken, guilt which comes from it, is what Christian metaphor terms original sin. Again, in terms of oedipal symptoms, there is also the belief in punishment by a parental figure, which again increases our fear on all levels. Any loss of oneness, any separation, brings guilt and fear, which gives us a mistaken foundation for belief systems based on fear and guilt. This begins at the primordial spiritual level and is passed to the soul and ancestral level, then onto our families, relationships and finally ourselves as individuals as it builds four distinct, powerful layers of separation, fear and guilt. Most people never get past the first layer of guilt to heal what we believe we did wrong and what we failed to do right. Relatively few people get to effectively deal with the second layer of Oedipal, family guilt, though all of us experience it. It is most rare for any to reach and heal the primordial guilt of belief in our separation from God or Oneness. One of the reasons the Oedipal is so difficult to resolve is that it has roots in our mistaken beliefs about our relationship with God.

At a subconscious level with a relationship heartbreak, there are feelings that we don't deserve to have the partner who left us, because of the mistaken childhood guilt of feeling that we stole away the parent of the opposite sex. We pay ourselves back when we feel we have betrayed our parents by setting up betrayals in relationships and career. This family layer of guilt is being fed by a spring of guilt from the spiritual level of the unconscious, where after leaving heaven's Oneness or dreaming that we did, we felt heavy but mistaken guilt from the belief we stole God's gift of creation and made this world of pain where we were trying to practise being God. This gave us the feeling that we killed God and that we've created a major enemy as a result. Believing God is angry with us allows us to remain in the illusion of separation and not take responsibility about what happens to us. As a result, we've closed the channel of grace and communication with God, making our own world, which includes hard work, suffering and death.

As I further studied the Oedipal Conspiracy I found that every conspiracy is made to provide for the ego's continuity by delaying, distracting, distorting or using any means to hold up our evolution. The ego's purpose in the Oedipal Conspiracy is to keep us stuck, separate from love, intimacy, sex, success, innocence, freedom, and other joining, ego-healing aspects. Like every conspiracy, the Oedipal is made to block and hide our purpose in life and our greatness. It keeps us frightened, hiding, feeling unworthy, reluctant to receive, and shrinking from our very selves. The Oedipal Conspiracy is generated from competition or lost bonding, and this has been passed from parents to children for untold generations. All of this keeps us stuck, believing there is not enough, while competing for what there is. It keeps us working hard to get what we feel unworthy to have. The ego uses a sacrifice strategy to hide and gives us a false sense of bonding with its use of fusion, all of this while attempting to cover over and pay off our guilt.

While the Oedipal goes on infecting much of our mind at many levels and layers, it can be dissolved by bringing the light of awareness and truth to it. The Oedipal Conspiracy can effectively block our love, success, abundance, sexuality and happiness, and given its pervasiveness, we are all at some stage of transcending or being trapped by it. The goal of this chapter is to bring awareness to the issue as succinctly as possible by stating the key issues involved so when symptoms arise, we can effectively begin to deal with it. For example, we may think we are dealing with having a new baby, being exhausted and staying up late while working all day and as if these factors weren't hard enough to deal with, the Oedipal can also become an issue with the birth of a child in setting up a competitive relationship. Sometimes all of the other symptoms are being driven by the Oedipal. We can experience hidden feelings of guilt buried from when we were a baby or child and our needs demanded attention and became competitive in a way which kept our parents apart. The only answer to all of the possible diverse symptoms of the Oedipal Conspiracy is continual awareness, joining and commitment to our partner to establish new levels in bonding. In this way our needs diminish, our bonding increases and the family reaches new levels of balance and cohesion. As a result, new levels of love and success are reached which we pass on to our children instead of this ancient illusion of the Oedipal Conspiracy, one of the best conspiracies the ego ever put together.

In any true, long term relationship both partners have the same level of Oedipal Conspiracy so while one partner may be having an affair as a symptom of the Oedipal, the other partner, by having this occur, may be trying to pay off childhood guilt that they betrayed one parent and stole the other. In problem situations both partners are equally afraid of the intimacy and sexuality which can come from an ever deepening relationship. Without bonding the Oedipal Conspiracy goes on to generate separation, fear, guilt, sacrifice, unworthiness, exaggeration and repression of sex, fantasy, temptation, competition, punishment and self-punishment, power struggle, deadness or lack of commitment which leads to affairs.

Here are some guidelines to explore as part of possible evidence of the Oedipal Conspiracy in our lives. All oedipal symptoms as they arise help to set up the other symptoms in a vicious circle. Symptoms build the conspiracy and are a result of it. Heartbreaks, starting with childhood, may be an expression of the Oedipal Conspiracy, with its fear of intimacy and its way of hiding competition, fear, shame and guilt about sexual feelings, or an attempt to pay off old feelings of oedipal guilt. Attacks given or received may be a possible expression of oedipal anger. For example, a man may have anger with his father or experience anger coming from his father as a result of the competition for mother and sister. Anger toward mother and/or her anger back is the need to push or be pushed away because of feeling too much guilt about sexual feeling or fusion, or both. On the other hand, guilt can come from being emotionally needy with our parents or being in competition for love and using withdrawal, or loss as a form of anger and a need to distance. Withdrawal from father, family, life, mother and sister can come from fear of anger and retaliation. Fusion with father or mother as the aggressor will occur to the extent that we give up our true selves. Competition can grow in the family especially with same sex siblings and parents. We use failure and betrayal by others to pay off oedipal guilt or the belief that we have betrayed others which can include school, career as well as relationships. Parts of ourselves which we reject, also known as 'shadow figures', can show up in dreams or waking life, especially that of the 'failure', 'the orphan', 'the thief', 'the murderer' and 'the betrayer'. Further evidence of the Oedipus Conspiracy can be fear of commitment, triangular relationships (especially if married people are involved) no relationship and even sexual fantasy.

It is also helpful to consider whether you were an oedipal winner or loser. If you were closer to the opposite sex parent than your same sex parent was to them, then you are an oedipal winner. This reflects how you usually get what you want but that you can't allow the final success or allow yourself to enjoy what you have received or accomplished. The oedipal loser who also did not come from a bonded family was not as close to the parent of the opposite sex. They're usually afraid to win or even have the drive to succeed as it is tantamount to winning the opposite sex parent. Oedipal losers typically don't succeed in life. Nowadays there is the beginning of evidence of families which are more and more bonded and balanced and where everyone is close and supports and enjoys the success of all family members equally.

Exercise

1. Awareness of the Oedipal Conspiracy:

- Tell your life story as an Oedipal Conspiracy. Use a tape recorder, a notebook or a friend. This will help you become aware of how you have used it as a way to hold yourself back from love, success, commitment, purpose, self,

greatness and your fear of moving forward.
- Now examine the Oedipal influence ancestrally. How did it seem to show with regard to your grandparents and your parents?

2. Steps to Resolve the Oedipal Conspiracy

- Awareness. Discuss the Oedipal Conspiracy with your partner or a friend as to how it may be affecting your life.
- Commitment. Commit to the healing of this conspiracy, both for the family you grew up in and your present family or relationship. Giving yourself fully is what the Oedipal Conspiracy attempts to prevent. Any place you give yourself fully or realise your fullness you obviate the Oedipal. Commit to your partner.
- Gifts. Imagine you brought in a gift to heal the Oedipal Conspiracy for your childhood family. Imagine yourself giving this gift or gifts to the family until they are all filled with it and free. Now, imagine it filling your parents and passing up through your grandparents, great grandparents, and on up to your ancestors, filling them and freeing them. Imagine sharing this gift or gifts with your partner and family now. Fill them up with it and free them. Notice how this establishes a new level of success and bonding.
- Will to be free. Refuse to be stopped by the Oedipal Conspiracy. Commit to awareness of this issue as the layers of it appear. Choose to

find all the ways through it. You will be inspired with different ways if you have the courage to listen for inner guidance.

- Centring. Go back to significant painful times in your original family and ask your higher mind to restore you and your family members to their centres. See and feel this effect of peace and grace on the family or relationship. Do this at least eight times, watching and feeling the effect on your family as it returns to each successive centre. This will effectively restore the bonding for the family at those times which will have many positive effects now. Do this if there were any painful, sexual events in your life. Again, after you ask to be carried back to each centre, notice the effect of it on everyone's behaviour. Do this with yourself and your relationship or your family now.

- Communication. Share with your partner about the elements you see affecting you. Every individual, couple and family has to face this, and as you share your awareness of this issue, you can build bridges to each other that are stronger than this ongoing conspiracy.

- Bonding. In your relationship now, imagine the light inside you joining with the light inside your partner. Experience the closeness and how it brings you to balance. Do this with all members of your present family. Finally do this with your original family. This exercise can be repeated as needed or for greater effect.

- Joining. Join with your partner heart to heart

and mind to mind. Go back to a significant time when the Oedipal Conspiracy was at work in your original family. Have yourself and everyone join to re-establish the bonding. See the effects of this on the family. Do more if it is needed until there is a deep bonding.

- Forgiveness. Any place you still experience loss or hurt, you haven't forgiven. Return to your original family's and your present relationships. Forgive them and yourself. You will know when you have succeeded by the peace you achieve. Forgiveness gives you and everyone ease and freedom, love and success which the Oedipal is meant to prevent.

- God's hands. Put your Oedipal Conspiracy in the hands of God. See what you're given in return for it. Do this with your original and present family. Do this for any partner, past or present.

- Commit to your purpose and embrace your destiny with all your heart. The Oedipal Conspiracy is meant to block your purpose, your destiny and your greatness as a child of God.

WAY 43 Embracing Grace

Any problem we have is at some level a result of trying to do it ourselves, instead of allowing for grace. Grace lets it be done through us, not by us. The problem could be handled easily if we received the guidance and help around, above and within us, but we've been following our own plan. The difficulty, hard work and effort of any problem is an attempt both to get attention and to prove we are good people. This lacks ease, effortlessness, inspiration and grace but the ego isn't especially interested in grace or ease because they belie the need for the ego. The ego is always quick to show how much it is needed to help us deal with problems, fear and the world. Yet the ego is always more concerned about getting and showing its best profile for its camera, than in actually resolving these issues. Our ego realises that if we fulfil our purpose, the promise we have made to help the earth, then we will have gone a long way towards recognising that the ego is not needed and is not our friend. It therefore convinces us that while we have a great purpose it is much too big for us and we might as well hide. We do have a great purpose, but the only way it can be accomplished is to have it done through us, not by us. The ego tries to do it by us, which makes it too big with too much work. When we start to live by grace we can do *so* much more, and in *so* much less time. Grace is God's Love for us. Grace is available to us in any situation. Whether it seems impossible or merely difficult, a problem is an illusion easily handled. If we are open to grace and include it in whatever we do, our lives become easy.

All too often, problems are the result of *our* plan for success which is, actually, a compensatory *busyness* which hides valuelessness. This doesn't lead us to success, it merely tries to prove we are not so bad. When a problem occurs we obsess about it, trying to find some way out of the trap. Yet the obsession is what blocks the intuition which gives us the answer. All of our *doing* demands more effort and eventually leads to difficulty because doing, which is not inspired, comes from an unstable place which lacks peace, grace and innocence. This means that we are in sacrifice, which not only blocks receiving, but also makes everything harder. Our *doing* and even our difficulty are attempts to prove we are good, worthy and useful, and are meant to hide our feelings of valuelessness. However, in spite of all our doing, feeling valueless is still a core belief, which is merely covered over and so we treat ourselves accordingly or work very hard to prove our value. In the midst of all of this valuelessness or busyness, we forget God and we forget grace, thereby living as if we have to do it all ourselves. We are afraid to let ourselves feel the valuelessness because when we do we feel tempted to die. Yet in feeling it we could make the choice for grace instead. Grace, a gift of God, establishes our undeniable worth as a child of

God. This has a way of easily healing the family patterns and dynamics where our unconscious levels of valuelessness are re-enacted and reinforced. Grace frees us of the need of spending years figuring out our problems.

Exercise

1. The antidote to your plan (which includes having to figure it all out yourself and work very hard for success or self-worth, hiding bad feelings which then doesn't allow them to be healed, self-attack, sacrifice and demand for others to sacrifice) is to simply ask your higher mind to show you the way. Sit quietly or meditatively and ask to be shown the way. You can also ask for a sign to show the way or to reconfirm that you are on the right track.

2. When facing any difficult situation, ask your higher mind to bring you back to your centre, or as many centres as is necessary for you to feel peace. Then, when you feel settled enough, ask for grace for whatever it is you are facing. Ask that it all be done through you, rather than by you. You can actually use this method to make your whole life easier. A key element to living in the mastery level of consciousness is that you live by grace, rather than by your own off-centred *doingness*. When masters are called to do something, they make choices with a clear mind about the ease and success of the event

or they don't even bother, knowing God has it handled. They let what they are called to do be done through them. This can turn what would have otherwise been extremely painful, stressful and exhausting situations into ones of ease and rejuvenation through grace.

Today commit to and receive grace. It will allow you to be effective not only for yourself but also for everyone else. From now on, take some quiet time to be open to the solution. Today, practise that everything be done through you, not by you. Let grace unfold every situation with ease for you in the best possible way and show you how to live in a whole new way. Ask heaven to handle any situation effectively.

WAY 44 Steps to Intimacy

When there is a problem in a relationship, and all situations are the result of relationships, then there is an agenda other than joining which is being dictated by our ego. This may be specialness, winning or attack, but whatever it is, it's a trap that holds us back. True intimacy is not special to one person because this closeness with someone removes fear. As intimacy grows with anyone, it grows with everyone, even those who have been enemies, victimisers or shadow figures for us. As we take a step in bonding with someone through joining mind to mind we also take a step forward in our lives. This both raises our consciousness and enables us to relate at a higher level to all those around us. Conversely, what we hold against anyone, we hold against ourselves and all others, as judgement and grievances build walls that separate us from everyone – even those we hold dearest. As our intimacy and bonding grow, so does our balance and understanding. And given that we are not enlightened yet, every problem which emerges provides a new opportunity for joining and a greater degree of balance and sense of wholeness.

As intimacy increases, so does awareness, because awareness and intimacy go hand in hand. The more we love someone, the more we see them without judgement and the more we see them in beauty. At times through intimacy it seems that we have the ability to see right inside someone, or know what they need, feel or think. With intimacy, we find others taking the words right out of our mouths or vice versa. Yet this can be done with anyone if we suspend judgement, look with compassion and peer into them lovingly. The more self-love or bonding we ourselves have achieved, the more connection we will have spiritually and the easier it will be to experience this level of connection and rapport with everyone. Though we have all probably heard that love is blind while marriage is a real eye opener, intimacy increases ease, bonding and awareness. Partnership is intended to help us grow in love as we learn our lessons together on the way home. Every conflict, fracture, withdrawal, separation or issue with anyone tends to come up with our partner, and as we subsequently heal and grow closer, more fractures within us come up as problems in the relationship. As we transcend the limits with new bonding our relationships become even stronger which provides the foundation to inspire and heal others. It also gives us the means of love and giving to be the star, genius or visionary we have come to be to help the world and light the way forward.

When two people, whether friends or spouses, have moved past power struggle and deadness in the relationship, they reach levels of partnership which increase creativity the further the couple goes along the path together. It is not that love is blind; in truth where there is love, we either overlook the mistake or we do not just see the problem, but go beyond it to the solution. When we do this we know we are not only joining with our partners but also with those around us working in concert with heaven to help. But we can only do this when we have let go of the guilt inside which makes us want to judge. Judgement pushes others away, destroying peace, dissociating and repressing what has been judged. This then places what is judged in the unconscious and projects a darker picture on the one judged, while we separate from them to show we are better than those we have judged.

Judgement always begins with ourselves and puts greater distance and conflict between us and our true selves and between us and meaning. With a lessening of meaning there is a growing sense of futility and stronger death temptation. Intimacy, on the other hand, provides meaning or rather discovers the meaning, which is always already there. The lines of bonding provide a certain level of safety and protection for those who are bonded, while creating greater ease to accomplish more.

Intimacy recognises as its enemies judgement, taking, guilt, loss, bad attitude, depression, attack, withdrawal, specialness, passive-aggression, fear, hurt, neediness, independence, control, dissociation, indulgence, stress, roles, self-concepts, burnout, deadness, holding on and expectations. As we cherish intimacy, we eschew these mistakes as lost opportunities for love and joining. We begin to patrol our minds for these feelings, beliefs and behaviours, as signs that we have chosen something we think is more important than intimacy.

Whatever we thought more important than intimacy, it did not bring us love and happiness. Since we know there is nothing more important than the intimacy which comes from love, joining, giving and forgiving, we begin to catch ourselves when we go down a negative path or obsession of any kind. We can then make another choice for the intimacy which would truly make us happy.

In the hustle and bustle of our everyday lives, we sometimes forget this crucial principle of intimacy and how it heals the loneliness, fear and separation which is part of the dynamic of every problem. As our relationship steadily grows, abundance, success, health, creativity, love, helping others and all the other gifts which provide meaning all steadily increase. When intimacy has become the main goal and deepest experience of our relationship with someone it will move us through thousands of relationship traps, making us that much more open and available to joining. This allows new levels of grace and heaven's love to become part of the equation of our love with not only our partner but with all human beings.

The ancient Hawaiians instinctively understood how the principle of intimacy could heal. A Ho'oponopono, a family gathering to bring about a new level of aloha, was called whenever a family member suffered a serious illness or accident. The family would paddle from the outlying islands to O'ahu, the gathering place, and the family elder or

Kahuna would conduct the Ho'oponopono. There was always lots of sharing and reconciliation until the family had once again achieved a level of unity. In most cases, as a result of the new level of joining and intimacy, the family member naturally or miraculously got better.

We have all heard that love heals, but we probably did not realise that it was practically possible for us to bring about enough love to help another. Through joining with our beloved or someone close to us, we can generate a level of intimacy for the purpose of love and helping another. This can bring about bonding and levels of transcendence, which at times seem miraculous.

Exercise

I shall present two exercises which are effective in building a new level of love and intimacy. As intimacy grows, problems melt away because at the root of every problem there is separation. The joining does not leave room for the hidden or not so hidden separation which gives rise to problems. Do not be surprised if another problem or another layer of the previous problem comes up. This is part of the human condition. Yet every time we heal ourselves we always move forward and as a result we have more of the courage and confidence, which allows for intimacy and success. Each problem is the next attempt by the ego to keep us separated, while for the soul it is our next opportunity to generate intimacy.

1. If your beloved or whoever it is you have chosen is available, ask them to stand across the room from you as far away as possible. If they are not present, you can just imagine their presence. Actually, the whole exercise can be done in your imagination if, say, you are in an airplane or some other such inappropriate place for actually acting out the joining. Commit to join whoever it is to establish a new level of intimacy and bonding. Imagine the distance between you and them as the meta-phorical distance needed to heal and bring a new level of love. Ask yourself what holds you back from your partner. As you discover each thing which keeps you from your partner, let it go. Take one step closer as you let each one go. Do this until you have finally let go of every thing which keeps you separated from your partner and you can embrace them. Besides the following suggestions of what could be in the way, be aware that your mind may intui-tively bring up some attack thought, hurt, temptation or fantasy as being in the way. Here are some common issues which come up between people:

- Let go of past grievances with your partner.
- Let go of present grievances with your partner.
- Let go of judgements on your partner.
- Let go of any past with your partner which is not happy.
- Let go of any place where there has been

inequality. Commit to your equality. This will release fusion, sacrifice and competition.

- Let go of any old wounds from your childhood which are now in the way between you and your partner.
- Let go of inequality with siblings, parents, teachers, coaches, past loves and peers from childhood adolescence. Commit to equality there at those times.
- Let go of any old wounds from your adult life that are now in the way between you and your beloved.
- Let go of inequality with siblings, parents, teachers, coaches, past loves, peers, and present partners in your adult life. Commit to equality now.
- Let go of your grievances with the opposite sex.
- Let go of your grievances with your same sex.
- Let go of any grievances with your mother or father.
- Let go of anyone you may be holding onto from family or old relationships. Attachments hold back present intimacy.
- Let go of any indulgences or addictions.
- Let go of any fantasies or temptations.
- Let go of any guilt.
- Let go of any expectations or 'supposed tos'.
- Let go of grievances from past relationships.
- Let go of attachments to something in a past relationship, either negative or positive.
- Let go of fear.

- Let go of the fear that you or they are not enough.
- Let go of the fear that it'll be so good you'll lose yourself.
- Let go of the fear of all the good things which seem overwhelming.

All of the above will block present intimacy. As you get close, you will probably notice other fears like the fear of 'melt down' or losing yourself. Actually you would not melt down or lose yourself; you lose a bit of the wall of separation which is the ego. Finally, there is typically the fear of that which we consider really good, such as intimacy, true love and having it all, love, and happiness. Let all of this go so you can join your partner. If your partner is actually present then it is their turn to stand across the room and do the same thing. If you keep your goal in mind during this exercise, such as increasing your love, healing yourself, your partner or a friend's problem, or establishing a new level of love, intimacy and ease in your relationship, it will make the whole process that much easier.

2. Look into your partner's eye. Left eye to left eye unless you feel the right is more comfortable. Feel yourself joining your partner heart to heart and mind to mind. Sometimes old pain comes up; just keep joining. Sometimes deadness or lack of feeling comes up; just keep

joining. Keep loving your partner, joining with them. Melt anything in the way, including defences, dissociation and deadness and anything between you and the love for them. Keep extending yourself energetically. This is not about romance or making out. It is the energy of love for everyone and everything. Join them energetically. Feel them joining you. If you make enough threads of joining, you will have a string. If you join enough strings, you will have a rope. Join a number of ropes and you will have a cable. Soon you will have a bridge of bonding between you. Sometimes you may find issues moving up your chakras or energy centres. This exercise may have different or more emotions as each layer of the problem melts away and the issues raise up to the next chakra, becoming more refined. Sometimes when you complete the healing at the end of a chakra, you may think you are complete, but then another layer shows up as you reach the next chakra. At the end of this exercise you will feel deep love and the sweet tenderness of having joined. You may melt away many layers which have not only stood between you and this person, but between you and everyone. It is possible to even raise the issue up through the seven chakras above the head. These are high levels of love and grace, and at the fourteenth chakra there is the experience of bliss.

There is always an element of the authority conflict in any problem. We attack someone for not being the leader that we want them to be, or for not following us in the way we want them to follow. This authority conflict can also reflect how we act as a follower. When we are afraid of freedom and of the natural authority which goes with it, we will attack authority figures as the ones holding us back, not realising the real block is our fear. We want to do it our way even when that way changes frequently, is difficult or even harms us. The rebel motto is: 'My way or the highway!' The rebel is based on the competition conspiracy, which has us compete against everyone – including God. This is such a pervasive conspiracy that we will heal layers of it all the way to enlightenment. Of all the shadow figures that I have worked on with people over the years, the rebel shadow figure was the deepest, most repressed and denied, and the last to give itself up for healing. The rebel gets us stuck in the trap of comparison and the vicious circle of superiority – inferiority. Superior people are compensating for feelings of inferiority and, on the other hand, if you question people about their inferiority, they admit with a 'busted' smile that they actually feel like they are the very best ones. This is a nasty trap which blocks bonding in the effort to win and be on top or to defeat another by being inferior. This sets up all manner of relationship problems and ineffectiveness at work.

In sacrifice, we are sacrificing ourselves to our partner, our family, society, God, as a form of avoiding ourselves, our purpose and intimacy. In the final essay our sacrifice shows itself as a form of the rebel by its avoidance of love, joining, purpose and destiny. In any form of rebellion, we are trapped in reaction but trapped nonetheless. We stay distant, dissociated and in conflict with whoever is the boss, because we want to be our own boss, or we stay independent to try to protect ourselves from too much pain and sacrifice. This is a result of burnout from family burdens, unmet needs from family or heartbreak in family and relationships. Now instead of sacrificing, we rebel. As the poet Richard Shelton described this type of relationship with his father, he was 'like a flag fighting its flagpole'.

When we fight to do things our way, our underlying complaint is that our partner, our family, society or God has done it wrong and now we will be our own boss and do it our way. The way out of this trap, which can go back and forth between sacrifice and burnout, rebellion then indulgence and burnout, rebellion, and so on, is to embrace partnership or leadership. Good leaders are by definition responsive to others' needs and good followers in response to others' leadership. In relationship we know that as we step forward and lead the way, our partner will automatically step up and receive the benefit also, unless our movement is a step away from our partner in power struggle or competition. If our partner steps up, we will receive the benefit automatically and gratefully by being moved forward, unless we are competing with them, in which case we will feel resentful.

With regard to our family we would be responsive and in service but without the sacrifice relationship based on fear. We would realise the importance of being true to ourselves while being helpful in a balanced way for our family. In society we would know that the only way to help is to be truly helpful and not fall for the trap of sacrifice or rebellion. Finally with regard to God, whom many think wants us to sacrifice, we would stop projecting our unworthiness, guilt and its demand of sacrifice on God. If a loving parent would not want their child to sacrifice themselves, it would be impossible for God to want this. Instead of sacrifice we would naturally become a teacher of God, love and grace, a source of inspiration and a resource for the world just by living a happy life and helping to free others. While accepting God's natural authority we become His hands and voice to help people remember love and God, not because we are preaching it but because we live it. Yet so many who project judgement on to God then see themselves as authorised to condemn, blame and attack in God's name. God by definition could not condemn, blame or attack. This surely does not have to do with what God wishes. This is ultimately based on our fear and attack and if we feel this we instil fear in others. Why would we frighten or condemn our own children unless we felt frightened and condemned ourselves? Certainly condemnation is not God's way, who would only want direct lines of love and communication with His children.

Many rebels begin reacting to religion and its followers. Many rebels fight with parents or teachers, who as a result of their own authority conflict became authoritarian and thus bred another generation of rebels. Many people who feel weak and fearful with regard to their own authority become overbearing in their office, using their title to give them importance, which generates resentment. Others in more important positions use their rank, role or God, country or company to lean on those below them. This is all part of how power struggle and competitive issues eat away at bonding. Co-operation, which brings success, results in people not having to fight society to find their way. All of us go through a dependent stage so we necessarily rely on others to take care of us. The extent to which our parents, teachers and religious leaders have authoritarian and competitive issues is the extent that there will not be bonding or where something more important than love will become the issue. This will then generate acting out and rebelliousness, especially as we get to the second stage of growth or independence. If we are not able to bond and join successfully we will not have successful lives. We will end up being a victim or victimiser or fail in work, relationships or family. We will then become authoritarian or controlling to the extent that we are emotionally arrested.

The way to step out of this trap is through bonding, right relationship and giving up the authority conflict for joining. With enough bonding we will naturally reach the partnership stage in relationships and then assume the leadership function. This allows us to work well with other leaders, to be a good follower when necessary and to step up and assume leadership when called.

By the time we have moved through the relationship stages of power struggle and emotional deadness into partnership, we have learned the value of putting the partnership before ourselves. We have learned to balance our needs, the needs of our partner and our relationship. We have given up dissociation for the most part to regain our heart and not be frightened of our own and our partner's past pain and either our own or our partner's needs are no longer so frightening. We have learned to value our partner and the relationship more than our specialness. We've given up narcissistic self-consciousness for a healthy awareness and willingness to reach out to our partner. We pass up taking and getting for giving and receiving. We by-pass neediness, sacrifice and the rebel for the joy of intimacy and the power of our relationship to generate success. We no longer desire to win without our partner but together.

As leaders we are already taking responsibility and caring for the group whether we are assigned or not. As leaders we step through the trap of sacrificing to society on the one hand or being rebellious to society on the other. We work for everyone's benefit. In giving up rebellion we are not just fighting against someone, we are following a path where we can lead society forward. To fight against someone makes them defensive, reinforces the problem we are fighting against, and makes it more real. Fighting invests in and reinforces the illusion there is something to fight against. As true leaders we don't attack or fight against, we look for the way forward, following the flow of inspiration. We don't carry others but influence and empower them to find a way through. As leaders we are carried by the flow of life, inspiration and the Tao, and are supported by those we support. Leadership does not carry others, that is one of the traps of leadership. True leadership finds a way through and maximises the inspiration, intelligence, play, enjoyment, and humour which refreshes and rejuvenates, knowing this will extend the flow and keep those following balanced, happy and motivated. No one wants to follow a sourpuss. We want to find someone who is visionary, irresistible with integrity, who cares about us, is committed to the goal and is efficient, brilliant and fun. Leadership plays a big game, working for everyone to win while effectively meeting the goal. Leadership empowers others to be their best selves.

On the other hand, the authority conflict is one of the roots of all problems. Feeling abused by authority, we don't want to accept any authority but our own. If we are authoritarian, we will be subservient and obsequious rather than helpful and responsible, until we take charge at which time we become overbearing, domineering and want others to do it our way. True leadership does not dominate or demand recognition, it inspires and empowers.

Another aspect of rebellion is that it may be an excuse to indulge ourselves in some way which can lead to addiction or even more sacrifice to pay off the guilt of indulgence, which then leads to burnout, rebellion and a vicious circle. While the rebel can be a true leader against fascistic, totalitarian, repressive or authoritarian regimes that are denying freedom, the problem is that as rebels we tend to get locked into that response and don't graduate to partnership, co-operation and true leadership. It would be as if we were arrested emotionally as an adolescent and didn't grow beyond this stage of development. All too often this is the case with certain character flaws. Because we were wounded by something we now remain rebellious and dissociated. What wounded us is seen as a *carte blanche* to act as we please. This is dissociated independence or rebellion and we are blind to its repercussions, such as difficulty in relationships. The rebel can be so strong as to keep us out of a relationship or once we have achieved a relationship, it can prevent or delay us from reaching for a successful bonded relationship until we give up the competitiveness that is incumbent with the independent or rebel.

Working hard without the ability to receive for what we have done is another symptom of this dissociation. Our rebelliousness tends either to not get us the recognition we desire or has us recognised in a negative way. Like anger the authority conflict is not discrete in that it affects every relationship we have, especially with our partner or even more our lack of a partner. This all comes down to a fear of losing our freedom, associating relationships with sacrifice and being told what to do.

This also affects our business relationships keeping us from partnership when this is called for and having us fight, confusing *our* truth with *the* truth, a common misunderstanding of independent people.

To the extent that we are not bonded we will have imbalance in our relationships which will show up as the roles of dependence, sacrifice and dissociated independence. This makes for painful, exhausting, difficult, dissociated or no relationships. In independence, however our relationships are, we tend to rationalise them or blame the other. For instance, a very independent person who enters a love relationship, can at times become dependent, chasing away a partner by needs and expectations and then stating that partners *should love and take care of each other*. While this goes against the principles of successful relationships, they will seek to rationalise their behaviour and deny their responsibility. They will then not learn the lesson necessary to succeed in a relationship which in this case is: needs are a form of taking which chases our partners away, no matter how we disguise it. Of course, as the rebel in the relationship we can easily become tired with another's dependency and leave, rather than transform the relationship.

The extent to which we have dependency and sacrifice is the extent to which we have hidden our rebellion. Dependence is synonymous with the victim because of the naive expectation for others to act in a certain way and meet our needs. Then with the hurt, heartbreak and revenge which occurs, it can lead us to become a victimiser, taking and disregarding others' needs or wishes because we regard our needs as more important. Or, having dissociated our own needs and pain, we are unaware of others' feelings, thus inadvertently hurting them.

Underneath all of our authority conflicts with partners, parents, leaders or bosses, is our authority conflict with God, the final authority figure.

Exercise

1. **Awareness** To be successful in healing the rebel you must first take an honest look at where you are in your life and growth. The most basic level of the rebel is the victim as blind follower, the one who gets constantly hurt, feels guilty and unworthy but judges and tries to make others live by ideals. This position, although it is not usually identified with the rebel, is actually the stage that sets up the rebel. Also, it is where the authority conflict especially shows itself in the lose-lose, win-lose and lose-win attitudes generating loss, heartbreak and guilt. In the second stage the rebel shows itself in its fashion of dissociation, expectations, perfectionism, holding on, control, power struggle, roles, deadness, burnout, no relationships, lack of recognition, overwork, busyness, lack of receiving for the amount of

work, dropping out, burdens, carrying others and general lack of emotion and enthusiasm. In the final stage there is at least success in work and relationship. Now we fine tune our game by examining the world around us for any form of the rebel as a reflection of our sub-conscious and unconscious, helping those who are dependent and victims, independent and dissociated, healing our shadow figures and any last bits of sacrifice, conflict, and dissociation. This is also where we head toward the higher end of interdependence (Vision and Mastery) having achieved a good partnership. As we keep going we give up dichotomy and the dualism of perception. We let go of doing for being, work for grace, choice for guidance, thinking for no-mindedness, unhappiness for joy, heaviness for laughter, and any last bits of prodigality for heaven's abundance. Once we realise where we are, making no excuse, we can choose and commit to live a more true, loving and bonded life.

There is one acid test for rebellion. The extent to which we are rebels shows at all levels of the mind by how little ease we have in our lives. The rebel stops joining, truth, partnership, co-operation, receiving and grace.

2. **Commitment** Today is the day to give up the rebellion, and allow answers to come in along with love, grace, help, healing, abundance, effectiveness and humour. Commit to the truth;

stop fighting yourself, those around you and God. This is a day to enter into bonded relationships of equality and to give up the Competition Conspiracy. Commit to partnership with everyone around you as a reflection of yourself.

3. **Prayer** Today is a day in which I am being asked to surrender to the love which surrounds me, from others and from God. Today is a day in which I commit to receiving help from those around me. Today I open myself for guidance, love and support. I will see and hear those around me today as speaking for the voice for God, helping, instructing and loving me. Today, I receive and accept this help with gratitude.

4. **Quiet Time** Spend some quiet time today listening with an open mind. Be aware today that messages may come in all manner of ways from the world around you. You know they're God's messages because of the love, grace and inspiration that will surround them.

WAY 46   Asking For A Miracle

Miracles suspend the laws of space and time and are part of our natural, spiritual inheritance. As children of God, we can ask for miracles. If we are willing to suspend the judgement which shrinks our minds and blocks the channel of God's love which generates miracles, then we can ask and they will be given to us. Miracles are gifts of love and signs of a higher order of reality which bring about more love, joining and forgiveness. In opening to miracles, we let go of judgement, fear and self-attack long enough to allow grace and truth to bring about this higher order. A miracle takes us out of seemingly impossible situations, affecting not only ourselves and others involved in our situation, but many like us in similar situations around the world.

A miracle takes us from our present perception and re-establishes the spiritual as the primordial reality. It comes through God's love for us and it goes out to others through us because of our love for them. A miracle transcends the fear of change that otherwise keeps us imprisoned in a lesser reality, and it is only when our fear of change is too great or our belief systems which we identify with would be too threatened, that miracles are not given. Miracles transcend our psychological fixations and remind us that under our many distractions there is an inexorable fixation toward God. Miracles show us that our prison door is open and freedom awaits because heaven's laws are ultimate. Miracles remove judgement, grievances, guilt, self-attack, sacrifice and the belief in the need for sacrifice and allow love to light up the world.

Since miracles are not self-generated, they naturally realign us as beloved children in oneness with God, our Father. There is no degree of difficulty of problems which a miracle cannot resolve. Miracles come from a wholeness of mind and restore the mind to wholeness, thus bringing about healing while transcending the perceptual realm. Miracles are available to us in all situations big or small, though sometimes we first need to purify ourselves. The guilt or unworthiness we believe in can all be turned over to our higher mind for transformational release.

A miracle is one of the best gifts we can give ourselves or anyone. It calls upon truth and allows us to change toward greater truth in an easy fashion. Our ability to invoke miracles has for the most part been repressed and relegated to the unconscious mind, but as we evolve toward radical dependence on God, miracles can once more become a natural and everyday part of our minds. A miracle is a collaboration between God and us for the benefit of others, which also greatly benefits us. Miracles come about through a medium of prayer in that we connect with God's love, restoring wholeness to ourselves and the situation. Miracles help us remember just how much we are loved. While others may be unaware of the possibility of miracles or just too frightened to receive them, we can do this for others making a natural bridge to them out of our love and friendship.

Exercise

Tonight, just before you fall asleep, and just as you wake in the morning, stop and feel God's love for you and everyone. Ask for and choose a miracle for yourself or for your friend(s). Every time the thought of a problem crosses your mind, make the choice for a miracle instead. Let yourself be included in God's love and share it with others.

Let love conquer fear and let yourself and your life be raised up. Let yourself be miracle-minded and trust the inspiration that calls forth your love to help. Trust also when you are not guided to help so you don't wear yourself out in trying to accomplish something where heaven has another plan. Most of all it's important to recognise that this transcendent power is a natural part of your mind and it can be embraced for your own and others' benefit.

Every morning when you wake up, ask heaven, 'What miracles would you have me do today?'

WAY 47   Friends Helping Friends

Friends helping friends is a concept which could change the world, and specifically your world. Imagine treating everyone as your friend as if their interests were yours. If we began to treat everyone as our friends, whether they lived next door or ten thousand miles away, the world would quickly change and grow into an ethic of sharing, co-operation, mutuality and teamwork. This would generate a shift in attitude to a higher way of relating, away from competition, win-lose, scarcity and the fear which all these attitudes engender. Bonding and its impact on love, success, abundance and ease would quickly become our goal and our way of life. The principle of friendship is its profound simplicity, which could generate such a vast and important change. Friends don't judge other friends. Friends see the calls for help and support their friends. Friends trust and are trustworthy. Friends are generous and helpful. Friends appreciate, enjoy and relax with their friends. Not everyone is a great leader, genius, visionary or even in a happy relationship, but almost all of us have friends in our lives who mean a great deal to us. We could extend this and be a good friend to everyone in our lives, to everyone across the world.

Friends helping friends is a principle which sees

everyone we come in contact with, and even those we haven't met, as our friend. We are willing to give to all others the same amount of love, warmth, help and support as we would to those closest to us. We would give the same amount of acceptance, tolerance, flexibility and bonding. This follows one of the great principles of happiness, which is to give rather than to try to get or take. In friendship we choose to extend ourselves rather than withdraw. We forgive rather than hold grievances. We look to understand rather than judge. We bless instead of curse. We delight in others and their success rather than disdain or resent. We cooperate rather than compete.

Taking this attitude of friendship to everyone in the world, we would learn to see all children as our children. We would cherish and love all those we came in contact with, treating everyone with honour and respect. The deep human needs for inclusion would be met, ending for the most part loneliness, depression, and scarcity. We would live lives where families were bonded rather than dysfunctional, where communities lived without the fear of crime because others would no longer be out only for themselves.

Buckminster Fuller, the American scientist, genius and visionary, proved scientifically that if everyone helped everyone else, in ten years the poorest person today would be richer than the richest person today. The world would change that much. He began to see as he studied the problem of feeding the hungry that there wasn't really a

scarcity problem in the world, there were distri-
bution and political problems.

Concepts provide the information to take us in
certain directions. Ideas that are inspirational
motivate us naturally to change. What will change
the world is an idea to which everyone can relate.
In spite of our diversity we will find common
ground. In spite of grievances we will seek reconciliation. In spite of differences we will bridge to
find greater integrity. We will realise that what separates us, weakens us and where we are joined we
are strong. We will move beyond all the issues of
race to one race – the human race. We will transform the trap of superiority and inferiority into
equality. We will move beyond a life of trying to
gain advantage to a way of life which gives advantage. We will begin to see all the nations of the
world as on the same team. We will stop looking
at money as the most essential goal and begin to
see happiness, the quality of life and raising the
level of consciousness and standard of living for
everyone as our main goals. When we give up the
eyes of judgement for the eyes of understanding,
when we give up trying to get and live by sharing,
when we recognise that the biggest challenge of
winning is to have everyone win, when we realise
that the answer to war is an investment and a
response in friendship rather than an investment
and response in the ego, then we will value peace
for the love and abundance it brings.

Friends helping friends is a concept which is both
inspirational and one to which everyone can relate.

It is practical, easy and unifying. Being truly helpful and in service is one of the best contributions we can make in life. It is purposeful, felicitous and care-free, relying on grace rather than the strain of serious effort. As we are helpful, we open ourselves to receive help so that in time of need, it is available to us.

We are never placed in a situation beyond us. Somewhere our giving is exactly what is needed to save the day. We can even learn to find the gifts needed within ourselves. If a friend is in need we can receive what they need through grace and share it with them. We don't have to know what to do or to say to help others, but if we are willing to give our help we'll be inspired with how to give it. People can get through anything with love and support. Our willingness to just show up and support can make all the difference. I have seen people survive living hells when there was someone there who loved and believed in them. A friend is someone who is walking in when others are walking out. Friendship brings fun, interest, humour, play, inspiration, intelligence, brilliance, tenderness, mutuality and bonding. These are aspects which generate flow, refreshment, happiness and rejuvenation.

Exercise

Today, practise seeing everyone as your friend. Give love, comfort and warmth to people you meet. Be truly helpful today. Be a friend to everyone around you today. Include your opponents. It will blow their minds and you will realise that they are a necessary part of your peace.

Spend a minute recognising those who need your help. Send them love. Call or visit them. Be a friend to everyone including yourself. Begin by blessing everyone instead of judging them. Commit to the idea of friends helping friends. Appreciate the friends you do have and the contributions which others make to you.

Today be the one to bring the humour, play and fun. Help and empower those around you. Delight in all you come in contact with. Join them in play and laughter. Would you choose to be a friend to life? A friend to the earth? When you finally leave your body, how many will speak of you as their best friend, someone who made a major contribution to their life? The world needs you. Your friends need you. See your interests as mutual. Give up the deadly indulgence of self-attack so you are not distracted from the calls for help which are occurring all around you.

WAY 48 The Path To Destiny

Just who do you think you are?! This is an age old question, sometimes used by others towards us with scorn. Who we think we are will be how we measure ourselves, our lives, what we aspire to and how we give ourselves to life and others. We spend our lives building up our self-esteem and working hard to maintain it, not realising that most of this is compensation for the deep layers of valuelessness, guilt and feelings of failure which came from our family dynamics. This led to a combination of independence from or sacrifice to our families. We carry these patterns into life, relationships and our own families unless we resolve them. This Family Conspiracy is one of the dozens of conspiracies we use to hide from our purpose and destiny.

Heaven has a plan for us, a destiny which does not contain either sacrifice or the burnout which comes from it, and leads to dissociated independence. Our lives are meant to evolve along a carefree path through stages of becoming and being and into Being. The more we are bonded the easier the evolution. I've seen evidence of this resistance to purpose and destiny in tens of thousands of minds around the world. We are frightened of our giftedness and greatness. And so we resist and rebel, not wanting to be told what to do, mistakenly thinking

that our true will is different than heaven's. We are
willing to use pain, problems and conspiracies
against ourselves so we don't have to listen. We want
to go our own way, following our ego's path and we
don't seem to care if this leads us into suffering and
pain. We think that our own autonomy is the most
important thing in the world and that without it we
would be mere automatons or slaves. But we have
confused resistance with our will. We think if we are
doing things our way it must be the right way or
the best way. Most of us celebrated a stepping into
independence from sacrifice, heartbreak and beliefs
where we just did what others wanted us to do,
doing what we were taught to believe as children.
So stepping into our own autonomy from family,
school, company, religion, government, country or
some ideology we had previously conformed ourselves to seemed like a good idea.

The more pain, loss, fear, hurt, heartbreak, guilt,
and sacrifice we had as children, the more this independence is dissociated and reactive. Unfortunately, all too many people stop at independence as
a place of resistance, reaction and rebellion. To the
extent we do this, we will be dissociated from hidden
needs, pain and negative self-concepts and we won't
know what it is we truly want because our energy
will be going into defence rather than into our true
direction. We will merely be in reaction to being cap-
tured and feeling enslaved again whether in relationship, work, or life in general. We think freedom
is a freedom from something, a reaction against, a
running away from rather than an opportunity, a

freedom to choose, a possibility to learn and develop
at a higher level and a chance to give and love more.
As a result we become competitive in relationships
to try and have our way be dominant. This leads
both to power struggle and deadness as we withdraw so as not to allow ourselves to be defeated.

When we finally graduate from this dissociated
and reactive independent stage we move into interdependence and finally we truly value joining, intimacy and partnership. This is a happier, more
successful stage and while we again deal with lessons
of dependence and independence we do it from a
higher perspective and a desire for more interdependence. It is at this foundation that we become
willing to explore and heal the unconscious mind.
But our evolution doesn't end in the stage of interdependence; we now begin to explore radical
dependence, the willingness to give up the ego-mind
for unity, enlightenment, and oneness. We realise
ourselves as a child of God deserving every good
thing. We stop valuing what is valueless. We become
disciplined in our thinking, realising that every
thought makes the world around us.

It is here we become masters on the way to the
realisation of enlightenment. We become active channels of bringing heaven to earth. We are willing to
have less of us and more of heaven. Our ego continues to melt away, leaving our true will, with its
power and joy. This is where our soul aligns with our
spirit, or the will of God. This is the beginning of
spiritual vision and perceiving the world in a whole
new way. As we recognise ourselves as children of

God, we begin to explore the consciousness of unity, which ties us all together. It is from here that we typically leap into enlightenment and though we could have done it sooner, we were distracted by ego and body interests. All of this is our destiny or who we came to be. If living our purpose fulfils us and makes us great, living our destiny brings us happiness and grandeur.

Our destiny is a place of love for all. We are full of happiness, grace, power and miracle-mindedness. It is a carefree and joyous place in which we once again identify ourselves with being, rather than with our doing. It is another step on the way to recognising ourselves as part of all Being or part of the mind of God.

Of course, most people never make it to anywhere near this level of consciousness though it is within all of us as our most essential part. It is here we can recognise ourselves as spirit, safe, pure, healed, and whole. While we are all called to reach this level, too many of us trivialise our lives and go off in false pursuits, after what can never fully satisfy us and think of ourselves as less than we are.

Between wherever we are in our present growth and where our destiny is, there is a path which is relatively carefree and happy. If we are not carefree and happy then we have obviously slipped off the path or gone on a path of our own. Even now heaven has a direct route from wherever we are now to our destiny. To keep us from losing our way too badly, wherever we have stepped off the path, heaven has now made it our path, part of the way home for us. In our fear we don't realise that our attempt for autonomy resists our real autonomy. Our egos have made up their own paths with their own agendas, to follow dreams of specialness. This, of course, not only delays and distracts us as we go off in frivolous or valueless pursuits, but many times also mires us down with problems because we are going against the natural flow of our own mind and heart. There are a few problems which are actually crucial lessons for our purpose and destiny. Most problems are fabricated by our ego to build itself up while holding us back from moving forward. After we have built up the ego's strength necessary for our growth and independence, to evolve we must begin to dismantle our competitive egos for the consciousness of co-operation, partnership, unity, union and oneness. This brings about greater love, joy and integrity with every step. It opens up and integrates all that we have repressed inside us. We have buried what threatened our egos from both our baser instincts and loftier aspirations. As we heal all our buried stories of horror, we let our experiences of light come back to us.

From wherever we are now on our path there is a next step. Each next step is always a happier and freer place, and so the ego sets a problem or temptation or both to hold us back. If we have a major or chronic problem in our way, what awaits us is a birth to a whole new chapter in our lives, if we have the courage to want it and will that it be so.

Our willingness, choice and commitment become some of the easiest ways to move forward. They resolve the fear and dissolve the present problem. While we could easily move ourselves out of problems by aligning our will with God's and our own true will, most of us are just grateful to move out of our present problems and then continue on with our ego's agenda. We don't see that problems are the ego's agenda, and though it has promised to get us out of problems, it does so in a desultory and incomplete way, usually getting lost along the way. Because the ego is the principle of separation and problems are a way of separating us from ourselves, others, and God, it is never committed to clearing our problems as it is tantamount to dissolving itself. Our ego promises us everything but works for itself and its own aggrandisement. Our own higher mind waits for our willingness to help us go as fast as we want through the mine field of our problems into greater peace, so that the path itself becomes carefree, easy and happy.

Exercise

1. Today be willing for the next step to come to you. It is a step which will come to you as a result of your choice and desire. Today be willing with all your heart. Resolve to be held back no longer. If you are in a chronic problem, wholeheartedly commit to the next chapter of your life. Every day and every time you think of this, with all of your heart *will* the next leap. One such sincere choice can change everything. Witness any changes which take place. You may

even want to keep a log or journal. If there is no significant change with a problem in two weeks then there's a hidden agenda – some attachment, indulgence or fear holding you back. Unless you're on the ego's path, life will continually get better.

2. Embrace your destiny and the radiance of your being. This commitment will accelerate your movement onto your true path. Want your destiny with your whole heart, as the best way to be happy and help the world.

The One You Can't
Forgive

The one you can't forgive is a judgement and grievance which sets up a corresponding problem or
series of problems in your life now. First of all, it is
important to realise that in the realm of healing,
there is no such thing as '*I can't forgive*'. There is
only '*I won't forgive*', or '*I refuse to forgive*'. In any
area where we have refused to forgive, our ego has
entrenched and defended itself. It is a place of ego-
centricity and victimisation, where we are frightened
and refuse to change or go on. It is important to
recognise that when there is someone whom we will
not forgive, there are other agendas going on such
as our desire to protect ourselves against our fear,
someone we are trying to defeat, some guilt we seek
to pay off, something we are trying to be right about,
someone we are getting revenge on, something
which gives us a life-long excuse not to show up,
change, learn, keep our promise, live our purpose
or embrace our destiny. It is a place which hides
some attachment or indulgence. But most of all
remember this: the attack of grievances is not discrete. It will punish everyone, including those you
love most indiscriminately.

In the area we refuse to forgive, we make continuous bad choices which constitute a bad attitude

in which we have mistakenly begun to move toward death. In whatever area of our lives this grievance occurs, our forward movement has become stuck. We are either heading towards life or death, and where we become stuck, we turn toward death. This is the same as believing we have sinned. In attempting to allay God's wrath, we punish ourselves. This occurs even if we don't consciously seem to believe in sin. Whenever we are caught in conflict, we have turned toward death because we are in an unliveable situation and we refuse to change.

Forgiveness takes us out of the hell into which we have locked ourselves. It is the solvent that releases the super glue of guilt which hides under our judgement and grievance. Forgiveness changes everything by freeing us and changing our perception of events. It refuses to let us hold anything against ourselves and as a result we also refuse to hold it against another. It releases us from the prison and the wound which the ego has used as a monument to itself and turns us back toward a life direction. It finally heals that conflict inside which could have killed us. When we have a wound we '*can't*' get over or have someone we '*can't*' forgive, we set up an oversensitive, narcissistic pattern of feeling wounded and rejected or in compensation we take on the need for control which rejects, demands and can wound. Because our wound has still not been accepted, we don't see a way through to move forward in that part of our lives. The wound gives us a feeling of specialness while at the same time making us overly self-conscious, but its attempt to take never satisfies us with real love or

allows us to move beyond ourselves to hear the calls
for help around us. It keeps us locked in the ego-
centricity of getting rather than the balance of self-
centredness, the centre of our true self in grace and
spirituality.

When there is someone we see as unforgivable,
we see ourselves as unforgivable in that same way,
although on the surface we may seem to act as if
we are superior. When we have judged another we
ourselves cannot escape that same judgement.
When we refuse to forgive it means the original
wound and stress of the event continues in our
mind as if it were still occurring. To be able to
stand the pain and stress, we build up lots of
defences and compensations. These blind us to our
feelings and needs and make us blind to the similar feelings and needs in others. In dissociating
from ourselves in an attempt to hide the pain, we
dissociate not only from those we love but also
from life itself. Our defences may hide the pain,
but they can never heal the pain. Our defences rob
us of the energy which we would use for responsiveness, love and happiness and we or our lives
become unresponsive, reactive or lacklustre.

In any refusal to forgive, our grievance generates a chronic problem. This becomes a trap which
turns into a conspiracy – a trap from which it seems
we will never escape. Where this has occurred, if
we want to free ourselves we must ask ourselves
how not forgiving this person *serves* us. How are
we using this victim event in our lives *now*? What
gift are we avoiding? What is it we don't have to

do as a result of this victimisation? By not forgiving, what fear are we mistakenly attempting to protect rather than resolve? What does it allow us to do? How are we using it to avoid our purpose and destiny? How do we get to be special? Who do we get to hold onto? What indulgence can we keep? What excuse does it give us? Where there is a chronic problem, there is someone we won't forgive and there is some ego strategy or agenda which we think will make us happy. Once we realise that our payoffs are not truly serving us, we can make a decision to find an alternative which moves in a life generating direction.

The key aspect of any ego agenda with regard to having a chronic problem or not forgiving someone is that somehow it is an attempt to make us happy. Even though this ego agenda may succeed in getting what we thought we wanted, it never brings us happiness. With someone we won't forgive, we are thrown into roles or dissociated life strategies, which actually keep us withdrawn from life or reactive to it. We believe we are on our own and as a result have to figure the way forward for ourselves. So we begin to believe either that there is no one to help or we must do it ourselves or we believe that we can't do anything ourselves and that someone has to do it for us. We give up on our own lives and instead lead lives of sacrifice. This is a classic ego suggestion which will only partially work to resolve the pain, fear, or guilt of a problem, but since the ego uses these very aspects to build itself up and keep its continuity, it never gives us an answer which would totally work. It is only when we begin to give up our allegiance to the ego that we begin to find our way to freedom. The ego wants us to live as if there were no God, no help, no guidance, and no grace. The ego wants us to believe that it is our only resource and that, as such, there is no other way and nothing else exists but the way it wants us to go.

Exercise

Imagine the one whom you will not forgive coming up to you. Ask them to forgive you. Yes, that is right, ask them to forgive you. See yourself getting down on your knees and begging for their forgiveness, saying '*I am sorry for using you to hold myself back. I am sorry I made you my excuse not to go forward and not to show up as if it were you, rather than my own fear which caused this. I'm sorry it was you whom I used as an excuse to throw away a precious and important gift, and to hide my life purpose of which I was afraid. I apologise for using you as the excuse to secretly indulge myself as I suffered with this chronic problem. Please forgive me, I will no longer use you to hold myself back. Forgive me for not seeing you needed my help. Forgive me for taking on your pain and passing it on to others rather then helping you. You reflect a part of my soul which I came to integrate and heal. I am now ready to heal it and I call on heaven's help to complete this forgiveness and free us both.*'

When they respond to your request, imagine yourself embracing them. See and feel the two of you joining and becoming free and whole in your joining, along with anyone onto whom you or they may have passed the pain or problem.

WAY 50 God

Whatever we believe about God will not affect how God is, but how God is for us. In our minds what we believe and how we experience is synonymous, though with even the slightest of openings a trickle of truth will come through to move us forward. I would like to approach the subject of God from reason and a psycho-spiritual perspective. This may not seem important to you, but I guarantee you that it is of infinite importance just on a level of personal growth alone. How we believe in God will be how we ultimately see ourselves as either guilty or innocent. This is a crucial factor in all problems, especially the mistaken, repressed guilt present in catastrophic illness. Many of us have closed down all channels to grace, to God's love, and we live hardworking, do-it-yourself, independent lives as a result. Most of us believe God doesn't really exist at least down on the level we are living. We are more vigilant for the things of the world than for God and His Kingdom. We may have done this out of reaction to religion and those who foster it. Or it may be a rejection of God on what we consider intellectual or humanitarian grounds because we hold God responsible for what is happening in the world.

As I have stated earlier, deeper than the family patterning that determines most of our lives there is the soul patterning which determines the family patterning and this is fundamentally all about our relationship with God. Most people never penetrate to this level of healing one's patterns or, as I've said in earlier chapters, most people never successfully get past the first layer of guilt about what they have done wrong or didn't do right. I shall present God in this chapter from my perspective as just another fellow traveller on the journey of life, but one who is ultimately concerned with freeing people and helping them transform their lives.

God is the Oneness of Love, Intelligence, Mercy, Power and Knowledge. Yet probably more people have been killed in God's name than for any other reason and certainly more is justified in God's name to give power to personal indulgence, domination, prejudice, judgement and cruelty. This is blatantly ridiculous and obviously dangerous. God is Love. Anything other than love is what humanity has made up and projected onto God and used as justification and excuse. The Bible can be read in a number of ways, either from a higher and more spiritual perspective or one used to justify one's actions for judgement, domination, control and revenge. For instance, 'Vengeance is mine says the Lord' can be read as God being vengeful or God wanting all vengeance to stop and be given over to Him. To project vengeance and judgement onto God is to put the psychology of an adolescent on the highest Being and Intelligence that exists, not to mention His Love and Mercy.

Over the years I have found thousands of people

who have repudiated the religion of their childhood because of the way some representative of that religion acted. Later as they realised that something was missing they went to another religion, found another spiritual path, or remained agnostic or atheistic because religion had been pushed down their throats. Some found another means to express their spirituality by altruism and service to humanity.

Studies have shown that as man evolved, so did his view of God. J.B. Phillips, in his classic book, *Your God Is Too Small*, carries this point forward. We have projected our own beliefs onto God, making God into our image rather than what He is. This has led to some rather strange theology. A California-based think tank reported its findings of how the idea of God has evolved from demanding ritual sacrifice of first-born children to the present day ideas of how we think of God. While I do not want to digress into what we have made out of God, I do want to address what seems to me to be some of the most blatant, illogical and destructive aspects of what people have pinned onto God.

It is easy to throw off God and religion altogether when people move from the dependent stage of growth into the independent stage of growth. Yet if we continue to grow and move forward we move into interdependence, and at this point we typically begin once again to embrace a more spiritual point of view even if it is not religious; that is, if we haven't done so already. The extent to which we partner with others, we partner with God, whether we call it that or not. But our relationships and consciousness will contain more spirit, love, compassion, creativity, grace, mercy, and so on.

We have deeply buried but strange notions about God. For instance, we believe that God wants to control us and have us do boring things. We think heaven is a dull place of lying around on clouds and playing obscure celestial instruments rather than the experience of Love, Joy, and Oneness. We think that God wants to imprison us, but He could no more imprison our will than His own since as the Principle of Freedom, He created us as free. Our love for God or for anyone can only come from freedom and choice. We attack God, fighting for our freedom with our pain because we think God wants us to sacrifice what we cherish in order to obey and follow Him. We think He'll take away our toys that we are afraid of losing, such as money, power, fame, success, sex, and possessions, but these are all just illusions in God's eyes. We usually use fear of what we'd lose as a way to separate ourselves from God, who is not interested in taking our toys away from us or in removing what we think is vital to our happiness. God just doesn't want us to hurt ourselves with these things or for us to think that they are what will save us or make us happy. As far as I can tell, the rebel archetype is the last major shadow figure between us and enlightenment, the realisation of our Oneness. It is the rebel who wants to stay separate, who has its own plan for happiness and who wants to fight God. The rebel in us also wants to blame God for what is happening in the world, so it can knock Him off heaven's throne and take over or, at the very least, do things our way – the right way in our rebel mind. Although these thoughts and feelings are in some of the deepest areas of the mind, their influences run all through our lives.

God does not judge, condemn, consign to hell, punish, torture, take vengeance, ask for sacrifice or place us in a position where we could fail. Imagine God as the most loving Father or Mother there ever was, having Love, Knowledge, Compassion and Wisdom. If this is so, how could God ever punish us? Punishment is a form of revenge that reinforces the mistake. This is bad psychology and at times just plain stupid. It simply could not be what God is about! Even a loving parent would merely want the child's mistake corrected, rather than watch the children attack themselves. Only guilt in a parent demands punishment rather than re-setting limits, helping the child face natural consequences but more importantly joining with the child to re-establish the bonding.

God does not fight evil or the devil. For there to be an opposite to God would mean that God is caught in polarisation, which is a level of consciousness that comes from our world of opposites. It is a lower form of perception we are all caught in until the higher stages of mastery or enlightenment. But if masters and the enlightened don't experience this polarisation or separation in consciousness, surely God wouldn't. God as a loving parent wants to help us out of suffering caused by living backwards, mistakenly thinking it would make us happy. The words 'evil' and 'devil' are the words 'live' and 'lived' spelled backwards. God would not fight an illusion. Psychologically, this reinforces it and gives it strength. God is just Oneness, nothing else. God continuously communicates the truth to help us and depending on our level of openness we are helped through our mistakes and temptations, which lead to guilt, being stuck, self-punishment, belief in sin, self-condemnation, attack, self-attack and the crucifixion of the body through suffering and painful death. God did not create sin, guilt or death. First of all, what is Perfect only experiences Perfection. God as Love creates us as love. God as Spirit creates us as spirit. Buddhism speaks of us being caught in maya, a dream or illusion that we think is real. We live in dreams, sometimes nightmares, which is why 'enlightenment' has also been termed 'awakening' and 'realisation'. God realises we are caught in dreams because we do not answer the forever call of communication and we no longer commune with God. We have forgotten who we are. We have forgotten our birthright and we have forgotten God. Even many of us who believe in God act as if He is not there and thus think we have to do everything ourselves. We have forgotten grace, given by our Loving Parent, who only wants to help us. This means we have unfortunately forgotten our very personal relationship with God and the practical help we could receive.

God is being framed. He is being blamed for everything done in the name of religion and its representatives. God is blamed for what we in our

free will have done. I have seen this as I have worked
deep in people's minds and helped them let go of
mistaken ego agendas and hidden selves that are the
reverse of what our conscious mind wants. Within
us there is tremendous fear which is the result of
experiencing God's absence or the even greater fear
of thinking God is attacking us, resulting from us
attacking God and seeing Him as an enemy rather
than a Friend. People carry repressed guilt from
childhood religious beliefs in sin, punishment and
fear of hell. The layers of guilt, sacrifice and self-
punishment which exist in the human mind and lead
to pain, suffering and tragedy are then attributed to
God and His Will, keeping us frightened of Him
and afraid to ask for help. If we know God as our
Loving Parent, our Friend, our Beloved, then we
would know that God would never do this to us.
God would not want us to attack and punish ourselves, just as we would not do this to our children
or want them to harm themselves out of some misguided notion.

If we use reason to examine this further we realise
that God, the Force and Source of Life itself, could
not create death. We who live in a world of polarity
think that if God created life then he also must have
created death. We believe that because we have identified with our bodies as ourselves, which causes us
great fear. God as Spirit created us as spirit. Those
of us who have had a near death experience know
that we have been just as aware and alive when
shucked from our bodies. The enlightened identify
with themselves as spirit. As God's children, we

could realise that our last name is God also and ask for the help and guidance which is the joy and pleasure of any parent to give.

When Lency's and my children were babies, our paediatrician, who was also an oncologist, said he had seen many types of parents – good, bad and indifferent. But he said he had never seen one who would not exchange places with their children when they suffered. God does not test us, wish us harm or want us to suffer or die. It is not God's will for us to live in scarcity when God is the principle of Abundance. If the Bank of Mom and Dad is good to us as children, how much more so is the Bank of God? Of course, like children everywhere, we sometimes have no idea of what is good for us, and have tantrums when something we want is taken away, but other than not being able to change the way it was established, God will not interfere with our free will because He trusts us. So if we want to suffer and die, it will be as we wish, especially if we have a hidden desire to suffer and die which is stronger than our desire for help. In tens of thousands of minds, including my own, I have witnessed harmful choices, mistaken strategies, destructive beliefs and idle wishes, which led to chaos, and conflicts that generated loss. We all have made mistakes, but there is help for us if we would but ask.

As a being we experience ourselves as separate from Being, and thus from all other beings, which is clearly impossible. As a being we proceed from and are an extension of Being. In the Bible, God throws us out of paradise, but God as God could never do this or even put us in a situation of failing if He is Love and Mercy. If it is paradise we cannot be thrown out, but we can leave, can go on strike or dream we did. In Being there is no loss of beings or they would wink out of existence. God cannot throw us out and keep the qualities of God; God would no longer be God. In leaving Paradise to try to be our own god we can project that God threw us out in an attempt to lessen our guilt while still keeping the separation. We are prodigal children but beloved nonetheless.

This original dream we fell into was one of separation, which led to fear, guilt and seeming distance between objects. In our need to displace our terrible but illusionary guilt coming from the separation, we projected it out to try and separate ourselves more from it. This made the experience of space. Time is the element that is then necessary to go from one place to another. More and more we fell into a bad dream of separation. The essence of the Bible in Genesis is our disobedience or making another will different than God's. Of course, this too is impossible; there can be no will different from God's, but we can dream there is. It was the primordial layer of guilt from believing we separated from God which directs the family guilt and major life patterns. In the depth I've explored, this was clearly a soul pattern, which set up the unconscious, sub-conscious and conscious mind patterns. Our family pattern is a compensation and a direct acting out of this pattern of authority, conflict and separation. It reflects in our families as lost bonding and conflict and the myriad roles and symptoms which result.

The original guilt we feel today, which is buried many layers deep in our psyche, is used for the purpose of keeping the original problem or the separation. Guilt allows us to avoid the lesson, not change, and keep whatever indulgence we want just so we beat ourselves up. At this deepest level we are all still afraid of healing this dream and realising oneness which is available to all of us all the time. We try not to have awareness of this because it would conflict with our ego's will, our experiment in building our own world and in doing things our way. The world is the reflection of our mind or our ego's will. It is a collective experiment in self-autonomy. The suffering, injustice, illness, hunger, scarcity and death by definition could not be God's will, if God was to retain God-like qualities, but they could be our will, which came about because of our need to rule ourselves. Naturally we might all begin to wonder how we could have got it so wrong, especially if we were made in God's image and likeness. This leads us inevitably to the authority conflict or 'who's in charge'. In our desire for self-autonomy we gave up Self-Autonomy. If we are God's creation, a child of God, then we are an extension of God and a part of His Love and Being. Yet in wanting to do it ourselves we had to leave oneness or dream we did. Even today we become frightened because our ego tells us oneness is some kind of totalitarian regime where we'd lose our freedom and that God is our oppressor. This is ludicrous for a couple of reasons. Firstly given how people act, we are all frightened of our freedom, so we project God taking away what we are trying to throw away or avoid. Secondly, God's Will and our true will must be the same. It is only in the ego's mind that it is different. Thirdly, God couldn't take away our free will, even to make the world better, even if He trusts us. If God stopped trusting us, we'd wink out of existence. Trust means we get to make our way and learn our lessons in this world. Yet, the more we embrace God the more help is available to us because pain, suffering and death could not be God's will for us.

So we fell out of Being or dreamed we did and set up time and space, which are both aspects of judgement. Separation and its incumbent judgement set up how much space there is between us and something else.

So as our soul explored through time we began less and less to rely on grace and heaven's help and more and more we shouldered the load in guilt, sacrifice, fusion and failure. This same pattern continues in our families at the deepest levels. Some of what we've come to heal within the family would be impossible without grace, without receiving the gifts that await us for every exigency we experience. In our most dire need its not that heaven deserted us but actually the other way around. We could still ask for help at any moment and receive it, if we didn't have the false fear of being told to do something we didn't want to do. What comes to us from guidance and grace reflects our true will and this lessens our investment in fear and in the ego and its ineffectiveness.

Typically we have no idea that what we hold against anyone, including ourselves, we hold against God. Our relationship with anyone reflects our relationship with God, and anything we think someone has done or not done for us is what we think God did at this deeper level of experience. This can become quite humorous when we realise what we're actually accusing God, the greatest force of Love, of doing or not doing. An example would be if we feel broken-hearted by someone leaving us, at a more primordial or spiritual level we feel God broke our hearts by leaving us or throwing us out of Paradise. God, of course, couldn't possibly do these things and remain God. If God is the principle of love, mercy and compassion, that which gives all to all, it shortly becomes evident that God could not possibly have done or not done what we accused Him of doing and remain God. Obviously, what we accused God of doing to us we've been doing all along to Him, namely leaving or abandoning God. We projected what we're doing onto Him and blame Him for all of our mistaken choices. If God did not remain God, everything would wink out of existence because the Ground of Being would be gone. So, if we think God is doing un-Godlike things to us, which is clearly impossible, then we must be doing it to ourselves. It stands to reason that if we 'reap what we sow', wnat is happening is what comes back to us from what we are doing as the result of our mistaken choices.

Yet, we are shy about examining our own minds

because as soon as we see that it is not someone else's fault, our ego attempts to slam us with guilt and make it all our own fault. The extent to which we are blaming God is how we have been blaming ourselves and if anything goes wrong we do blame God – but this is buried under our blame of others. This self-attack and self-condemnation which the ego uses against us when we stop blaming others, is one of the best weapons the ego has to keep us from exploring our minds, taking responsibility and making another choice. If anyone is to blame, underneath, we blame ourselves and we are trapped in what we have judged as we have judged it. If we think God is to blame, we attack our God-self or spirit, blocking grace, help and guidance. God as Innocence created us as innocent. We have made many mistakes and existentially we do experience guilt. If we understand that this guilt is ultimately not the truth, we can recognise that it is our ego reinforcing the mistakes, while we use our guilt as an excuse not to give up a certain indulgence. We deny or hide the indulgence from ourselves, all the while making a big show of beating ourselves up.

Judgement or self-judgement prevents us from learning the lesson involved and serves as a barrier between us and others while keeping us in conflict. This could never be God's Will for us, as any suffering is not God's Will. Any loss is not God's Will for us. Death is not God's Will for us, but part of our own hidden agenda. Any loss is not God's

Will for us but our own projected rejection of something we no longer value. God as Life could not will death, pain, conflict, disappointment, bitterness and tantrum, which frequently accompanies death. To receive God's peace, love, grace and all the gifts God wants to give would move us beyond the traps in which we have been caught. We could live a beautiful, carefree, happy life helping others until we awaken. Fear would be gone from our lives as we realised the presence of God as a loving Parent. We would embrace God's Will for us, which contains only happiness, success, love and creativity.

Exercise

1. When anything negative occurs in your life state, 'This is not God's Will for me and neither is it my will. This is not what I want. I somehow made a mistake in what I chose. Now I want to find the fastest and easiest way out of this to achieve success and I ask this with all my heart.'

2. Imagine yourself with your problem stepping into an elevator and the elevator going down and stopping in your subconscious mind. How does your problem look and feel in there?

    Now imagine that the elevator is moving down to your unconscious mind. How does your problem look and feel to you here?

Now sense your elevator going down to the part of your unconscious mind which holds miracles. How does your problem look and feel to you in this part of your mind?

Now experience your elevator going down to the part of your mind which is the super conscious mind, spirit and light. How does your problem look and feel to you now?

After a while, feel your elevator going up once again to the miracle part of the unconscious. How does your problem feel to you here?

In a while, see your elevator going up to the rest of the unconscious mind. How does your problem seem to you now?

After a pause, listen as your elevator moves up into the subconscious again. How does your problem seem now? What are you saying to yourself about your problem now?

Finally, come up to your conscious mind. How are you and what has happened to the problem?

3. Place your problem, your fear, and your future in God's hands. What are you given back for it?

• Close your eyes and repeat the name of God quietly. Do this for 5–20 minutes. Feel any feelings which come up. Continue till you feel in a deep state of peace.

• Think of your problem and repeat the name

of God, not in-vain, until your problem seems
to melt away.

- During the day, every time you think of it,
  repeat the name of God as a mantra in the
  back of your mind.

Glossary

Readers who are new to the concepts in this book might find helpful the following explanations for some of the most commonly used terminology.

Bonding The connection that exists between us and others. Bonding creates love and success with ease rather than with struggle and difficulty. It is what gives cohesiveness its glue and teamwork its mutuality.

Compensation What psychologists call 'reaction formation'. It is a role that is meant to hide and make up for negative feelings, and it is meant to prove that we are positive, innocent and deserving of love. When there is compensation present, we act in an opposite way, as a reaction to a mistaken feeling. However, it doesn't allow us to receive because it is not true giving. It is a mechanism of proving. Unfortunately, much of what we do can be considered compensation. But it's a wasted effort and an attempt to prove what doesn't need proving – namely our innocence and value.

Conspiracy A chronic trap of the ego, set up so well that it looks like we will never escape it. Conspiracies are particularly difficult to heal until we realise that the problem has been set up that way.

Ego The part of us that seeks separation and specialness and – ultimately – wants to be God. It is the part of us that fights for itself and its own needs first. It is built on fear, guilt, negativity, and competition, wanting to be the best of something, even if it is painful, or the best of the worst. Ego distracts, delays, and attempts to stop evolution, being more concerned with its own continuity. It is based on domination-subjugation, rather than any form of strength or truth. It is ultimately an illusion. We make it strong, while we are young, and then melt it away for partnership and grace.

Fusion A muddling of boundaries that occurs when bonding is lost. We cannot tell where we end and another begins. Fusion is the ego's answer to the lost intimacy. It is counterfeit bonding, which creates sacrifice and builds resentment. Fusion sets up an overburdening sense of loyalty. This eventually causes us to burn out and move into the opposite extreme of independence. We move from over-caring and smothering to acting as if we do not care.

Gifts Aspects of greatness or grace that make any job easy. Our gifts are the answer to all situations because they remove the problem. Gifts are learned lessons that continuously give and create flow. They are packets of wisdom, healing and responsiveness for the situation at hand. In every problem, there is a potential gift. We have thousands of unopened gifts within us that are the antidote to pain and problems.

Higher Mind The aspect of the mind that is creative, contains or receives all of our answers, and opens our will and our spirit to the grace that heaven and the world around us wants to bestow on us. It is always guiding us with a quiet voice toward the truth. It encourages us to win together, not only now, but in the future.

Love The ultimate goal and the best means to the goal. It is the sweet fulfilment that comes of an open-hearted extension of oneself. This is the giving, receiving, sharing and reaching out to one another. Love is the foundation of being and the best description of God, whatever your religious beliefs. It gives us everything we want – meaning, happiness, healing, nurturing, and joy. Our evolution and happiness are based on how much we give and receive in love.

Manifest Consciously using the mind to choose what we want. It is the use of visualisation, feeling and sensing what we want, and then letting it go and trusting. It allows us to create exactly what we want in detail.

Sacrifice A psychological mistake in which we give and don't receive. It's a role that compensates for feelings of failure, guilt and unworthiness. It hides competition and taking, and it attempts to lose now to win later. A script of sacrifice tells a story of us losing for others to win at a time when a script could be written for everyone to win. Sacrifice is afraid of the intimacy that brings equality.

Scarcity A fear-based belief that there is not enough and that we, or someone else, will have to go without. A belief in scarcity sets up power struggle, competition and sacrifice.

Shadow Figures Self-concepts that we have judged about ourselves and as a result, repressed. They represent areas of self-hatred that we project out onto others around us or onto the world in general.

Tantrum A choice in which we react, complain, withdraw or hurt ourselves when life does not come about as we consciously want. It can show itself as any form of failure, immaturity, or lack of success.

The stages of relationships
Although this book is not specifically about relationships, all of life is based around them. It is useful to understand the stages we go through, in order to understand where we stand with our partners and in our own minds.

All relationships go through stages on their way to making heaven on earth. Each stage has its own challenges, traps and answers. If you know the stages of relationship, you are better prepared to handle the challenges and not to be blind-sided by the issues.

1. Relationships begin in the Romance or Honeymoon Stage, where we idealise the other, yet it is in this stage that we can see and feel the potential of the relationship.

2. Then there is the Power Struggle Stage where we are learning to bridge our differences, communicate, join and integrate both positions. Here we project out our shadow figures on our partner, and primarily fight for our needs.

3. The Dead Zone is a stage where we are learning to transcend good form for authenticity, find our worth without roles or sacrifice and learn how to bond, moving beyond the counterfeit bonding of fusion.

4. The Partnership Stage is where we have reached a balance between our own masculine-feminine sides and, correspondingly, we do so in our relationship, with our partner, finding balance, equality and intimacy.

5. The Leadership Stage is where we have both become leaders in life and have learned to value each other beyond the conflict and competition of personalities.

6. The Vision Stage occurs when we have become a visionary along with our partner, making contributions to the earth and healing unconscious pain and fractures.

7. The Mastery Stage of relationships is where we have healed our feelings of failure and

valuelessness to the point of moving from doing and becoming, to being and grace. This is where we become living treasures to the earth. It is the beginning of heaven on earth for our relationship.

Further Information

PSYCHOLOGY
VISION.

For details on other books, the full range of audio and videotapes, and world-wide seminars, please contact us at:

Psychology of Vision UK
France Farm
Rushall
Pewsey
Wiltshire SN9 6DR
UK
Tel: +44 (0)1980 635199
e-mail: promotions@psychologyofvision.com
website: www.psychologyofvision.com

Also by Chuck Spezzano
(and available from the Psychology of Vision):
The Enlightenment Pack
Awaken the Gods